6/11
3.43
n

D1482517

perfectly *plus* ™

Nobles County Library
407 12th Street
PO Box 1049
Worthington, MN 56187
31315001904171

HOUSE of
WHITE
BIRCHES

PUBLISHERS
SINCE 1947

Introduction

. . . .

It is time for chic, full-figured women's garments. A well-fitting garment does not have to be expensive; it needs to be flattering—flattering for the wearer's body shape, size, and to some extent, her age group.

Emotionally attached to size, conquering the "numbers" may not be an easy task. Quite frankly, ready-to-wear clothing in larger sizes is often less marketed, has fewer choices, is less colorful and less flattering.

Although we know this to be true in off-the-rack garments, there is every reason to have hand-knit garments that fit. The fitting tips found in this book will provide the opportunity to have knit garments that not only fit, but are fashionable and figure-flattering.

Table of Contents

Skipping Stones,
page 28

Make Me Blush,
page 32

Dappled Shadows,
page 36

Ipanema,
page 53

Swing Along,
page 48

Savoir-Faire,
page 40

Creating Knits That Fit

The Fitting Process

In order to have a properly fitting garment, we need to start with the basics. Gauge is the most important factor in getting a proper fit. Secondly, an accurate set of measurements is required. Within the measurements, chest and shoulder widths are crucial. The exercises that follow will guide you to your current measurements—where to take them and how to take them. Make time annually to get a new set of measurements.

Learning this method for personalized fit, on the Simply Fitting Shell, page 21, and Simply Fitting Cardigan, page 24, is only a beginning. This system can be used on most knitting patterns and for any individual.

Fitting tips and instructions precede the individualized calculations (in green). Calculations are italicized. The standard shell and cardigan patterns are bolded; your individual pattern is in violet. If no violet appears, use the bolded pattern. Assumption of general knowledge of knitting abbreviations is made.

Gauge

Gauge is the most important thing to understand. Without proper gauge or consistent gauge, a garment will not fit properly. You MUST do a gauge swatch. The swatch should be made in the pattern stitch as pattern gauges vary. If there are several patterns within a garment, swatch each of them. The recommended minimum size is 30 stitches over 25 rows. This is not meant to be discouraging, but it is important to make a large enough swatch to show consistency in stitching. If the garment is knit in the round, the swatch should be knit in the round.

While half of a knitting stitch does not sound like much, the difference of half a stitch per inch compounded over the entire garment is amazing.

Example:

5 sts per inch on 100 sts = 20 inches and would make a 40-inch chest.

5½ sts per inch on 100 sts = 18¼ inches and would make a 36½-inch chest.

How to Adjust Gauge

Adjust the needle size. Rule of thumb: one-half stitch per inch for every needle size.

For example, 5 sts per inch on size 7 (4.5mm); 5½ sts per inch on size 6 (4mm); etc.

Referring to your swatch, fill in the blanks in the chart below. The gauge, both rows per inch and stitches per inch, and needles used for the swatch are necessary. Guessing is a liability.

YARN: Name/Color _____ Manufacturer _____
MY GAUGE: _____ sts per inch and _____ rows per inch
MY NEEDLES: US# _____ for ribbing (smaller) and
US# _____ for body (larger)

Choosing Size

With a basic tape measure, measure your chest at its fullest part. If in doubt, take two or three measurements and use the largest number. Measure your hips at their fullest part. This may be 7 or 9 inches below your waist, and again, you may want to take several measurements.

When choosing the proper size for your garment, the amount of ease desired needs to be calculated. Ease, in the case of sweaters, refers to the fit of a garment. A tight-fitting sweater has *negative* ease. Socks and gloves are examples of knitted pieces which require negative ease. Conversely, a looser fitting garment has *positive* ease.

The Craft Yarn Council guidelines specify ease as follows:

Very Close Fitting—Actual chest/bust measurement or less

Close Fitting—1–2 inches larger than actual chest/bust measurement

Standard Fitting—2–4 inches larger than actual chest/bust measurement

Loose Fitting—4–6 inches larger than actual chest/bust measurement

Oversized—6 inches or more larger than actual chest/bust measurement

Ease plus chest measurement = Finished Chest measurement (fill in the green blanks for your measurements).

$$\underline{\hspace{3cm}}" + \underline{\hspace{3cm}}" = \underline{\hspace{4cm}}"$$

inches   inches   Finished Chest
                                    measurement

Finished Chest Measurement divided by 2 = Finished Piece measurement.

$$\underline{\hspace{3cm}}" \div 2 = \underline{\hspace{4cm}}"$$

inches   Finished Piece
                              measurement

The Craft Yarn Council has provided some of the measurements used in this book. We have added additional ones to help with the fitting process.

Using the chart below, find the closest actual chest size. Either highlight or circle the selection.

Begin Adjustments
Note: *The finished chest/bust number for the shell will probably be smaller than the finished chest number for the sweater, due to ease, even though they will be worn by the same person.*

The additional measurements that need to be filled in are:

Shoulder width—From tip of shoulder, across the back to the tip of other shoulder. The shoulder width for the shell may be smaller than the shoulder width for the cardigan. It all depends on where you want those shoulders or shoulder seams to end.

The Simply Fitting Shell, page 21, is written with **Close Fitting** ease. The Simply Fitting Cardigan, page 24, pattern is written with **Standard Fitting** ease.

How much ease do you desire?_____"

	1X	**2X**	**3X**	**4X**	**5X**
SIZING STANDARDS FOR PERFECTLY PLUS All garments designed for 5'6" height					
Bust	44–46"	48–50"	52–54"	56–58"	60–62"
Hips	46–48"	52–53"	54–55"	56–57"	61–62"
Shoulder to shoulder	17½"	18"	18"	18½"	18½"
Armhole depth	8–8½"	8½–9"	9–9½"	9½–10"	10–10½"
Underarm to wrist	17½"	18"	18"	18½"	18½"
Upper arm (circumference)	13½"	15½"	17"	18½"	19½"
Center back neck to cuff	31–31½"	31½–32"	32½–33"	32½–33"	33–33½"
Back waist length	17¾"	18"	18"	18½"	18½"

Fill in actual body measurements (in inches) on the schematics below.

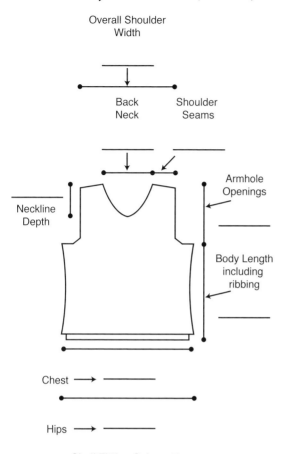

Shell Fitting Schematic

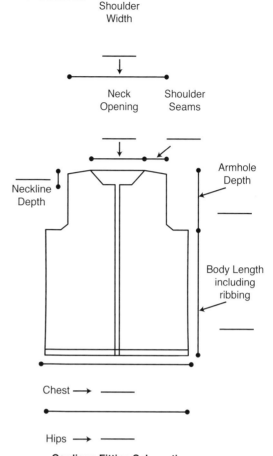

Cardigan Fitting Schematic

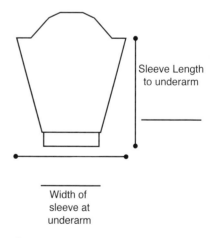

Cardigan Fitting Sleeve

Length of shoulder seams—Measure from base of neck at side to tip of shoulder, excluding armhole trim. Again, the shoulder seams for the shell may be smaller than the shoulder seams for the cardigan.

Neckline opening at back—Measure across the back base of the neck to those points where you want the neckline to open, exclude neckline trim (a good standard is 8 inches).

Desired neckline depth—Excluding neckline trim, measure depth vertically from top of shoulder seam to bottom of desired neckline on front.

Armhole depth—Measure individually for both shell and sweater as they will be different. Measure vertically from tip of shoulder to top of bra at your underarm for shell; measure 1–2 inches deeper for ease in cardigan.

Body length—Including ribbing, measure from underarm to desired length of garment.

This is all about your comfort, so make the adjustments you desire.

Yardage Calculations

Knitting can be a wonderful leisure activity, but on occasion, we frustrate ourselves. Have you run out of yarn before the project is completed, or have you had so much left over your "stash" begins to grow? We've all done it.

A quick way to estimate yarn is to break the garment into pieces. The front and the back for the shell are pretty easy. Adding sleeves? Long sleeves should take approximately as much yarn as the back; short sleeves, half that much.

To determine if more yarn is needed, some simple calculations are needed.

Total recommended yardage for desired size, as noted on pattern: _____ yards

Divide that by either 2 (sleeveless), or 3 (long sleeves): _____ yards

Note: *For a short-sleeved garment, an extra step in calculating is needed. Using the resulting number from the overall yardage divided by 3, take that number and divide it in half.*

Example: 1,500 yards total needed for long-sleeved sweater. Divide by 3 = 500 yards each for back, front and sleeves. Then divide the 500 for the sleeves in half; 250 yards are needed for the short sleeves.

Determine the percentage of either increase or decrease to the body length of the garment. Using the same formula, calculate the difference in percentage of yarn needed for the sleeve adjustments.

Example:

15 inches		17 inches (new length)
100%	x	N% (new percentage)

Therefore, 17 x 100 = 1,700 ÷ 15 = 113.3333%

With the new length (rounded up is 114 percent), 14 percent more yarn will be needed for the front and 14 percent more for the back.

Calculate the yardage for the front, back and sleeves separately. Add those adjusted yardage numbers together to get the overall adjusted yardage for the garment.

Divide the overall adjusted yardage by the number of yards in the chosen ball/skein of yarn. This will give the number of balls or skeins needed for the adjusted garment.

Do I Need More Yarn?

Yardage for nearest size to mine = _____

I changed the pattern _____ percent
longer/shorter.

*Add or subtract percent to or from original yardage
estimate. Divide new number by number of yards in
skein/ball.*

Number of skeins/balls needed _____.
(Always round up if the number of skeins/balls
is fractional.) ●

Make-it-Fit Basic Shell

Back

Determine the style of the hem ribbing. Usually the proportionate number of stitches in the ribbing to the garment is 90 percent, using smaller needles. There are several options for adjusting the ribbing for a less-snug fit.

- The first and easiest option is to cast on the same number of stitches as the body of the garment, and work the ribbing on smaller needles. This will still be smaller than the garment body.

- The second option is to use the larger-size needles and cast on the same number of stitches as the body of the garment. This will be slightly smaller than the alternative above.

- The third option is to use the larger-size needles and cast on 10 percent more stitches than needed for the body of the garment. Most instructions will say to increase a certain number of stitches after the ribbing is complete. In this option, decrease that same number of stitches before starting the body of the garment.

Since these garments are worked from bottom up, if the hip measurement is significantly larger than the chest, use the hip measurement for the beginning cast-on calculations. Decreases may be made at the sides for a better chest fit. Conversely, if the chest is significantly larger than the hips, a smaller number of stitches may be desired to cast on, with increases made along the sides to accommodate the chest.

Gauge times ½ total Finished Hip measurements = sts in body (remember, no ½ sts in cast on).

_____	x	_____	" ÷ 2 =	_____
sts		inches		sts in body (hip)

Cast-on sts times percentage (number of ribbing sts to body sts—more ribbing sts is over 100%) = total sts cast on.

_____	x	_____	% =	_____
st		percent		sts cast on

With _____ size needle, cast on _____ sts.

With smaller needles, cast on 103 (111, 121, 129, 139) sts.

Determine the type of ribbing (1x1, 2x2, etc.) to be used and the length of ribbing. Fill in the blanks.

Work _____ type ribbing for _____".

Work in k1, p1 rib for 2½ inches.

Ribbing to body increase

If the desired ribbing is 10 percent smaller than the total number of stitches needed for the Finished Chest, this is the time to increase the number of stitches for the body of the garment.

Stitches needed for half Finished Body size (previously calculated) minus Ribbing Stitches = total number of stitches to be increased or decreased. Divide the number of Ribbing Stitches by the total number of stitches to be increased or decreased. Don't worry if there is an uneven number. On the last stitch in the sequence, work the increase stitch by knitting in front and back of that stitch.

_____	-	_____	=	_____
sts		ribbing		sts increased/ decreased

Ribbing stitches divided by increased/decreased stitches = number of sts in increase/decrease repeat.

_____	÷	_____	=	_____
sts		sts		sts in repeat

Example: 110 sts for Finished Body size minus 99 Ribbing Stitches = 11 sts needed for increase.
  Divide 99 sts by 11 (increase sts needed) = 9 (number of sts in increase repeat) [Knit 8, knit in front & back of next st] 11 times. There will be 110 sts.

On next ribbing row, work inc as follows: [Work

_____ sts, k1fb] _____ times, evenly spaced

across row. [_____] sts. (If decreases are neces-

sary, use k2tog instead of k1fb.) Change to larger

needles if necessary and St st. Work 1 RS row.

On next ribbing row work inc 12 (14, 14, 16, 16) sts evenly across row. There will be 115 (125, 135, 145, 155) sts. Change to larger needles and St st. Work 1 RS row.

As the body of the garment is being worked, adjustments may be made with the stitch count to accommodate either smaller or larger chest. To determine the number of stitches either increased or decreased, *subtract the chest stitches from the hip stitches.* This is the number of stitches that need to be either increased (larger bust) or decreased (smaller bust) from the first row of stockinette stitch.

Chest measurement plus ease divided by 2 = Finished Chest size for piece.

(_____" + _____") ÷ 2 = _____"
   inches   inches   Finished Chest/Piece

Finished Chest size for piece times gauge = sts at chest.

_____" x _____ = _____
   inches   sts   sts at chest

Sts at hips minus sts at chest = sts to be increased/decreased.

_____ - _____ = _____
   sts   sts   sts increased/decreased

Divide stitches to be increased/decreased by 2 to determine the sts to be increased/decreased on each side.

_____ ÷ 2 = _____
   sts   sts per side

It is here that, in most patterns, adjustments for length are made. Measure the desired underarm location to the desired length of the garment (body length). The underarm location will be lower on the sweater than on the shell due to the greater ease in the sweater. You may also want to make the shell slightly shorter than the cardigan.

Subtract the ribbing length from the desired garment body length to determine the length within which the increases/decreases need to be made. Divide that remaining number by the number of stitches to be increased/decreased.

This provides the spacing in inches between increases or decreases. It is better to have a few rows left in stockinette stitch with no increases/decreases than to run short. If in doubt, err on the side of finishing increases/decreases short of the underarm length.

Inches for Finished Body Length minus inches of Ribbing Sts = length for increased/decreased sts.

_____" - _____" = _____"
   inches   inches   working length

Length for increased/decreased sts divided by sts to be increased/decreased per side = spacing between increases/decreases.

_____" ÷ _____ = _____"
   inches   sts   between
                              shaping sts

Every _____" increase/decrease 1 st each side.

Body shaping

The Simply Fitting Shell, page 21, has a bit of shaping in the body. Using your gauge of rows per inch, divide in half the number of rows needed for the length between the end of the ribbing and the beginning of the armhole decreases. Usually there are 3 decreases and then 3 increases for a slight waistline shaping. Depending on how much waist shaping you desire, you can work more decreases with corresponding increases. Just space them out evenly within the rows.

Number of shaping decreases/increases

desired _____.

Length between ribbing and armhole decrease times gauge (rows) = number of rows for shaping.

$$\underline{\hspace{2cm}}" \times \underline{\hspace{2cm}} = \underline{\hspace{2cm}}$$
inches   rows   rows for shaping

Divide the number of rows for shaping by the number of shaping decreases plus increases to get the number of rows between shaping stitches.

$$\underline{\hspace{1.5cm}} \div (\underline{\hspace{1.5cm}} + \underline{\hspace{1.5cm}}) = \underline{\hspace{2cm}}$$
rows   decreases   increases   rows between shaping sts

At the same time as hip/chest shaping, dec 1 st each side every _____ row _____ times. Then, inc 1 st each side every _____ row _____ time(s). (_____) sts.

Continue in St st until piece measures _____" from beg.

Dec 1 st each side every 12th row 3 times. Inc 1 st each side every 12th row 3 times. There will be 115 (125, 135, 145, 155) sts.

Continue in St st until piece measures 16 (16, 16, 16, 16½) inches from beg.

Armhole shaping

We will determine the shaping of the armhole by using your measurements and a bit of math. Remember to allow for 1-inch armhole trim. The armhole width and depth will be custom fit for you. Begin the armhole shaping by making the following calculations:

Finished Chest divided by 2 minus Shoulder to Shoulder Width = desired armhole decrease amount in inches.

$$(\underline{\hspace{1.5cm}}" \div 2) - \underline{\hspace{1.5cm}}" = \underline{\hspace{2cm}}"$$
inches   inches   inches armhole decrease total

Multiply armhole decrease total by the gauge, then divide that number by 2 (for each armhole) to obtain number of sts in each armhole shaping.

$$(\underline{\hspace{1.5cm}}" \times \underline{\hspace{1.5cm}}) \div 2 = \underline{\hspace{2cm}}$$
inches   sts   sts in single armhole shaping

Example: Subtract 13 inches (shoulder width) from 20 inches (half the Finished Chest size) = 7 inches. 7 inches times 5 st/in = 35 sts. 35 sts divided by 2 = 17½ sts. Since the number is a fraction, round down and put that extra stitch in the neckline. By this example we need to decrease, from the beginning of the armhole bind-off to the shoulders, 17 stitches on each side.

Half of those decreases should be in the armhole bind-off, the other half should be along the armhole edge.

Stitches in one armhole shaping divided by 2 = number of stitches in bottom armhole bind off.

$$\underline{\hspace{2cm}} \div 2 = \underline{\hspace{2cm}}$$
sts   sts bottom armhole

Divide number of stitches in bottom armhole bind-off by 2 to get the number of sts to be bound off in each of two rows (no partial stitches again, so use larger number on first bind-off row, smaller number on second bind-off row).

$$\underline{\hspace{2cm}} \div 2 = \underline{\hspace{2cm}}$$
sts   sts bound off per row

Example: 17 stitches need to be decreased on each side. 17 sts divided by 2 = 8½ sts. If the number is a fraction (as in this case) round up to get the number of stitches in the armhole. In this example it would be nine. Nine stitches makes for a rather abrupt armhole bind-off. Divide those stitches roughly in half. The armhole bind-off in this example will be: Bind off 5 sts at beg of next 2 rows. Then bind off 4 sts at beg of following 2 rows.

Finished now with the first half of the decreases, the second half of the numbers, eight in this example, need to be decreased along the armhole edges while working up the piece.

Hint: *Add a locking stitch marker on one of the stitches. This will make it easier to measure the distance from the armhole shaping.*

Bind off _____ sts at beg of next 2 rows. Bind off _____ sts at beg of following 2 rows. Dec 1 st every RS row _____ times. Continue in St st until piece measures _____" from armhole bind-off (refer to schematic for armhole depth).

Bind off 5 (5, 6, 7, 8) sts at beg of next 2 rows. Bind off 4 (5, 6, 7, 8) sts at beg of following 2 rows. Dec 1 st every RS row 8 (10, 11, 13, 15) times. Continue in St st until piece measures 8 (9, 9½, 10, 10½) inches from armhole bind-off.

Calculate the number of stitches remaining after armhole bind-off.

Chest stitches minus total armhole (both sides) decreased stitches = remaining stitches after armhole shaping.

$$\underline{\hspace{4cm}} - \underline{\hspace{3cm}} = \underline{\hspace{5cm}}$$
sts   sts   sts remaining after
                              armhole shaping

Shoulder and back neck decreases
Look at the worksheet schematic. Calculate the neck opening in number of stitches. Remember to allow for 1-inch neck trim.

Back neck opening times gauge = stitches in back neckline.

$$\underline{\hspace{4cm}}" \times \underline{\hspace{3cm}} = \underline{\hspace{5cm}}$$
inches   sts   sts in back neckline

Number of stitches remaining after the armhole shaping minus the number of stitches in the back neckline divided by 2 = number of stitches for each shoulder shaping.

$$(\underline{\hspace{3cm}} - \underline{\hspace{3cm}}) \div 2 = \underline{\hspace{4cm}}$$
sts   sts   sts for
                              shoulder shaping

For graded shaping, divide the total number of shoulder bind-off stitches by 3 to obtain number of stitches per bind-off row. If the number is not divisible evenly by 3, extra stitches will be added to the first and second bind-offs.

$$\underline{\hspace{3cm}} \div 3 = \underline{\hspace{5cm}}$$
sts   sts per row
                    (plus extra sts to make total)

Bind off _____ sts at beg of next 2 rows. Bind off _____ sts at beg of following 2 rows. Bind off _____ sts at beg of next 2 rows. Put rem _____ sts on stitch holder for neckline.

Bind off 7 (7, 8, 8, 8) sts at beg of next 2 rows. Bind off 7 (7, 8, 8, 8) sts at beg of following 2 rows. Bind off 7 (8, 8, 8, 8) sts at beg of next 2 rows. Put rem 39 (41, 41, 43, 45) sts on stitch holder for neckline.

Front
Work the same as the back up to the armhole shaping. On the first bound off row of armhole stitches, work approximately halfway into the row, place a locking stitch marker here, continue armhole shaping.

Hint: Adding a locking stitch marker on one of the stitches will make it easier to measure the distance for the neckline shaping. On a scoop-neck sweater, stitch markers may be added on each side approximately a quarter of the way in from each end of the row. Remember, it is only used to determine length not number of stitches.

Neckline shaping
To determine the neckline depth, place a long strand of yarn around the back of your neck letting the ends hang down over your chest. Place a ruler or other straight edge horizontally across your chest at your most comfortable neckline depth. Measure the length of yarn from your shoulder to the point where the yarn and the ruler meet to give you the neckline depth. Remember to adjust for 1-inch neckline trim. To determine the length from the initial armhole to the beginning of the neckline shaping, *subtract the neckline depth (measurement just taken) from the overall armhole length (on schematic).* The remaining number will be the number of inches from the beginning of the armhole to the beginning of the neckline shaping.

$$\underline{\hspace{3cm}}" - \underline{\hspace{3cm}}" = \underline{\hspace{4cm}}"$$
inches   inches   inches from
                                  armhole bind-off

Measure the horizontal distance between the two strands of yarn.

Multiply this distance by the stitches per inch in the gauge. This is the total number of stitches needed for the scooped neck.

$$\underline{\hspace{3cm}}" \times \underline{\hspace{3cm}} = \underline{\hspace{4cm}}$$
inches   sts   sts for neckline
                                  scoop total width

A scoop neck requires adjustment for even and gradual shaping. The bottom scoop width is often the width of the base of your jaw.

Multiply the number of inches (of jaw width) by the gauge.

$$\underline{\hspace{2cm}}" \times \underline{\hspace{2cm}} = \underline{\hspace{3cm}}$$
  inches   sts   sts at bottom of
                               neckline for holder

This measurement and stitch count may be adjusted for personal preference.

   Start with a smaller number in the center, then decrease in multiples of 2 stitches on each side of the neck opening for a few rows. This will make the scoop wider and more gradual.

Number of stitches at bottom of front neckline plus any stitches used for scoop shaping minus the number of stitches at the back neck, divided by 2 = number of decreases at each neck edge that need to be made along the neck fronts.

$$(\underline{\hspace{1.5cm}} + \underline{\hspace{1.5cm}} - \underline{\hspace{1.5cm}}) \div 2 = \underline{\hspace{2.5cm}}$$
   sts   sts   sts   sts to be
                                     decreased at each
                                     front neck edge

Example: 3-inch width at base of neckline depth. 3 times 5 (stitches per inch) = 15. Place 15 stitches on stitch holder. 15 bottom stitches plus 8 (gentle scoop) = 23 stitches (overall scoop at neckline depth). 40 stitches from back neck minus 23 stitches in overall scoop = 17. 17 divided by 2 = 8½. But, there are no half stitches in actual knitting, only in gauge. Adjust the number of stitches placed on the holder by 1, making 16 stitches on the holder. 16 plus 8 = 24. 40 minus 24 = 16. 16 divided by 2 = 8. Decrease a total of 8 stitches each side of the neckline.

Work same as for back, including all shaping. At the same time, when the piece measures _____" from armhole bind-off, work to center _____ sts. Place center sts on stitch holder. Attach another ball of yarn and work to end of row. Work both sides at the same time.

Work same as for back, including all shaping. *At the same time*, when the armhole measures 4 inches, work to center 13 (13, 13, 15, 15) sts. Place center 13 (13, 13, 15, 15) sts on stitch holder. Attach another ball of yarn and work to end of row. Work both sides at the same time.

For scoop shaping, bind off _____ sts at each neck edge _____ times. Dec 1 st at neck edge every RS row _____ times.

Bind off 2 sts at each neck edge 2 times. Dec 1 st at neck edge every RS row 7 (8, 8, 8, 9) times.

After all the decreases have been made, continue in St st, if necessary, until the armhole for the front measures the same as the armhole for the back.

Continue in St st until armhole measures 8 (9, 9½, 10, 10½) inches.

Shape shoulders
Work shoulder shaping to correspond with the back.

Finishing
Block both pieces. Sew shoulder and side seams. Before sewing up the side seams, slip the garment over your head. Double check the shoulders are going to fit right. Have someone help pin the side seams and check for armhole depth and looseness. It would be better to find out fitting issues now rather than after the rest of the finishing has been done.

Neckband
With smaller circular needle, beg at left shoulder seam, pick up and knit at a rate of 3 sts for every 4 rows along left neckline, pick up and knit sts from front neck holder, pick up and knit 3 sts for every 4 rows along right neckline, pick up and knit sts from back neck holder. Work in k1, p1 rib for 1 inch. Loosely bind off all sts.

Armhole band
With smaller circular needle, beg at underarm seam, pick up and knit underarm bind-off sts, pick up and knit at a rate of 3 sts for every 4 rows around armhole, pick up and knit rem underarm bind-off sts. Work in k1, p1 rib for 1 inch. Loosely bind off all sts.

If the armhole openings are still too large on the shell, there are a couple of remedies.

   The easiest way to fix this is to run some matching elastic thread around the armholes.

   However, the best way to correct this is to take out the armhole band. Go back to where the pick-up sts in the underarm were completed, and pick up and knit 2 out of 3 rows around the armhole. Depending on your personal shape, you may only have to adjust this pick up for front or back only.

   Weave in tails. Lightly reblock if necessary. ●

The Make-it-Fit Basic Cardigan utilizes all the fitting principles of the Make-it-Fit Basic Shell, with only a few modifications and the addition of sleeves.

Gauge requirements are necessary. Check yours, especially if the yarn you're using for the cardigan is different from the shell. Before beginning, make yardage calculations to prevent surprises. If the gauge and needles are different for the cardigan, place the new information in the chart below.

YARN: Name/Color _____ Manufacturer _____

MY GAUGE: _____ sts per inch and _____ rows per inch

MY NEEDLES: US# _____ for ribbing (smaller) and US# _____ for body (larger)

Unlike the Simply Fitting Shell, page 21, written with close-fitting ease (1–2 inches), the Simply Fitting Cardigan, page 24, is written with standard ease (2–4 inches). Taking into account the adjustments needed for more ease, write your new numbers in the appropriate spaces on the cardigan schematics on page 7.

Note: *Remember to lower armhole shaping by 1 inch for ease. (Shorten the body 1 inch, and lengthen the armhole 1 inch.)*

The fitting process for the shell provided the opportunity for individual tailoring. The cardigan includes only individualized fitting instructions not previously covered. Please refer to the pages 5–14 for help, as necessary.

The new numbers can be obtained by simply adding the amount of additional ease to the existing numbers for the widths of the shell (hips, chest, etc.). **Note:** *The ease is for the overall garment. Divide the numbers in half to get the measurements for the back, or by 4 for each front.*

The additional ease added for the shoulder widths and armhole depths is not quite as large a number as adding to the width. Measure your shoulder and armhole depths again, keeping in mind the need for additional ease. The rule of thumb on this is about ½–1 inch more in overall shoulder and/or armhole measurements.

One huge difference between the shell and the cardigan is the addition of sleeves. There are some extra measurements to account for by the addition of sleeves.

First, measure your sleeve length. This should be measured from the wrist (or your comfort sleeve ending) to the beginning of the underarm armhole shaping. Before adjusting the sleeves of the sweater, determine if it is the sleeves that need adjusting or if the concern lies in the shoulder width. This is a very common problem for knitters. Shoulders that are too wide will still make the sleeves too long, even with multiple measurements and knitting the sleeves to an exact length.

The second part of the sleeve that will cause problems for many knitters is the circumference of the sleeve at the armhole. Often times this part of the sleeve is way too tight. There are a couple of different ways to accomplish this adjustment. If the problem is between the wrist and the beginning of the armhole/sleeve cap, add a few more stitches in the increase above the cuff, then add a few more stitches to the sleeve shaping increases. Work those extra stitches in the armhole bind-off and sleeve-cap shaping, adjusting the rate of bind-off to shorten the sleeve-cap so it will still fit into the armhole.

If the additional circumference needs to be added to the upper arm, one option is to make the armhole opening larger. Adjust the number of stitches in the sleeve shaping increases. Work those extra stitches in the armhole bind-off and sleeve-cap shaping. The sleeve-cap height may not need to be adjusted to accommodate this longer armhole length.

Back

The cardigan has ribbing around the lower edge. To prevent the "lightbulb" look, the ribbing for the cardigan is worked with 10 percent more stitches than needed for the hips and is worked on the larger-size needles. After the ribbing is worked for 2½ inches (or desired length), stitches are decreased evenly spaced across the row.

Gauge x (½ x total finished hip measurement) = number of stitches in body.

Note: *Remember, no half stitches in cast on.*

_____ x (½ x _____") = _____
    sts   inches   sts in back body
                                           (hips)

Number of stitches in body x percentage = number of ribbing sts to cast on.

Note: *Ten percent more ribbing stitches are added to the total stitches cast on.*

_____ x 110% = _____
   sts   sts cast on

With _____ size needle, cast on _____ sts.

With larger needles, cast on 132 (143, 154, 165, 176) sts.

Work _____ type ribbing for _____ inches.

Work in k1, p1 rib for 2½ inches.

Ribbing to body decrease

On next ribbing row, work dec as follows:

[Work _____ sts, k2tog] _____ times, evenly spaced across row—[_____] sts. Work 1 RS row. Refer to calculations on previous page and on Basic Shell pages.

On next rib row work dec 12 (13, 14, 15, 16) sts evenly across row. There will be 120 (130, 140, 150, 160) sts. Work 1 RS row.

Continue in St st until piece measures _____ inches from beg. Refer to Basic Shell pages for calculations, remembering to account for ease.

Continue in St st until piece measures 16 (16, 16, 16, 16½) inches from beg.

Armhole shaping

Bind off _____ sts at beg of next 2 rows. Bind off _____ sts at beg of following 2 rows. Dec 1 st every RS row _____ times. Continue in St st until piece measures _____ inches from armhole. Bind off (refer to schematic for armhole depth). Refer to shell workbook for calculations.

Bind off 4 (5, 7, 8, 9) sts at the beg of the next 2 rows. Bind off 4 (5, 6, 7, 8) sts at beg of following 2 rows. Dec 1 st each end of every RS row 8 (10, 12, 14, 17) times—88 (90, 90, 92, 92) sts. Continue in St st until armhole measures 8½ (9, 9½, 10, 10½) inches.

Note: *There is no back neck shaping in this pattern.*

Shoulder shaping

Bind off _____ sts at beg of next 2 rows. Bind off _____ sts at beg of following 2 rows. Bind off _____ sts at beg of next 2 rows. Place rem _____ sts on st holder for neckline. Refer to shell workbook for calculations.

Bind off 8 (8, 8, 8, 7) sts at the beg of the next 2 rows. Bind off 8 (8, 8, 8, 8) sts at the beg of the following 2 rows. Bind off 7 (8, 8, 9, 10) sts at the beg of the next 2 rows. Place rem 38 (40, 40, 42, 46) sts on st holder for neckline.

Right front (make left front, reversing shaping)
When calculating this, allow for 1½-inch button band (2nd button band overlaps so it does not have to be allowed.)

Back cast-on stitches minus (1½ inches times number of gauge stitches) divided by 2 = stitches to cast on per each front section.

_____ - (1½" x _____) ÷ 2 = _____
   sts   sts   front cast-on sts

With _____ size needle, cast on _____ sts.

With larger needles, cast on 66 (71, 77, 82, 88) sts.

Work _____ type ribbing for _____ inches (match back).

Work in k1, p1 rib for 2½ inches.

Ribbing to body decrease

Number of stitches decrease on back divided by 2 = total number of stitches decreased.

$$\underset{\text{sts}}{\underline{}} \div 2 = \underset{\text{sts to be dec}}{\underline{}}$$

On next ribbing row, work dec as follows: [Work ____sts, k2tog] _____ times, evenly spaced across row—[_____] sts. Work 1 RS row. Refer to previous calculation above and those on Basic Shell pages.

On next ribbing row, work dec 6 (6, 7, 7, 8) sts evenly across row. There will be 60 (65, 70, 75, 80) sts. Work 1 RS row.

Continue in St st until piece measures _____ inches from beg (as for back).

Continue in St st until piece measures 16 (16, 16, 16, 16½) inches from beg.

Armhole shaping

Bind off _____ sts at beg of WS row. Bind off _____ sts at beg of following WS row. Dec 1 st every RS row _____ times. Refer to calculations for back.

Bind off 4 (5, 7, 8, 9) sts at beg of WS row. Bind off 4 (5, 6, 7, 8) sts at beg of following WS row. Dec 1 st end of every RS row 8 (10, 12, 14, 17) times—44 (45, 45, 46, 46) sts.

Continue in St st until piece measures _____ inches from beg of armhole shaping (allow for ease).

Continue in St st until armhole measures 6 (6½, 6, 6, 6½) inches, ending with a WS row.

Neck shaping

Refer to shell workbook for calculations, note that cardigan has higher neckline. Remember to allow for 1-inch neck band.

Bind off _____ sts at beg of next RS row.

Dec 1 st at neck edge, every RS row _____ times.

Continue in St st until piece measures _____ inches from armhole bind-off (refer to schematic for armhole depth).

Bind off 12 (13, 10, 11, 12) sts at the beg of the next RS row. Dec 1 st at neck edge, every RS row 7 (7, 10, 10, 11) times—25 (25, 25, 25, 23) sts. Continue in St st until armhole measures 8½ (9, 9½ 10, 10½) inches.

Shoulder shaping

Bind off _____ sts at beg of next WS row. Bind off _____ sts at beg of following WS row. Bind off _____ sts at beg of next WS row. Refer to Basic Shell pages for calculations.

Bind off 8 (8, 8, 8, 7) sts at the beg of the next WS row. Bind off 8 (8, 8, 8, 8) sts at the beg of the following WS row. Bind off 9 (9, 9, 9, 8) sts at the beg of the next WS row.

Sleeve
With smaller needle, cast on 47 (51, 55, 59, 61) sts. Work in k1, p1 rib for 2½ inches, ending on a RS row. Inc 5 (7, 7, 7, 7) sts evenly spaced across the next row. There will be 52 (58, 62, 66, 68) sts. Change to larger needles and St st.

Sleeve shaping
Many people adjust sleeve length. Measure from the underarm armhole to the desired length of the sleeve at the wrist, including cuff. This is the length of the sleeve to the beginning of the armhole shaping. Adjustments may need to be made to get the required number of increases into the new sleeve length.

If there is a need for an increased arm circumference in the sleeve, adjustments can be made in two places:

* If the problem is between the wrist and the beginning of the armhole/sleeve cap, add a few more stitches in the increase above the

cuff, then add a few more stitches to the sleeve shaping increases. Work those extra stitches in the armhole bind-off and sleeve-cap shaping, adjusting the rate of bind-off to shorten the sleeve-cap so it will still fit into the armhole.

- If additional circumference is needed in the upper arm, make the armhole opening larger. Adjust the number of stitches in the sleeve shaping increases. Work those extra stitches in the armhole bind-off and sleeve-cap shaping. The sleeve-cap height may not need to be adjusted to accommodate this longer armhole length.

Sleeve increases should be completed approximately 1 inch before the armhole.

From the length of the sleeve (beginning of cuff to armhole bind-off), subtract 2½ inches (cuff length plus 1 inch from armhole shaping). This number is the number of inches within which the sleeve shaping needs to be worked.

$$\underline{\hspace{2cm}}'' - 2\tfrac{1}{2}'' = \underline{\hspace{3cm}}''$$
inches   inches to make sleeve shaping

Take that number times gauge (rows) for the number of rows available for the increases.

$$\underline{\hspace{2cm}}'' \times \underline{\hspace{1.5cm}} = \underline{\hspace{2.5cm}}$$
inches   rows   rows available for increases

The first increase needs to be made at the first (or possibly 2nd) row of the stockinette stitch in the sleeve and a final increase 1 inch before the armhole.

The fullest part of the arm plus ease multiplied by stitch gauge = the maximum number of sts for the sleeve.

$$(\underline{\hspace{1.5cm}}'' + \underline{\hspace{1.5cm}}'') \times \underline{\hspace{1.5cm}} = \underline{\hspace{2cm}}$$
inches   inches   sts   sts in sleeve

Stitches in the sleeve minus stitches at the beginning of stockinette stitch = number of stitches to be increased.

$$\underline{\hspace{2cm}} - \underline{\hspace{1.5cm}} = \underline{\hspace{2.5cm}}$$
sts   sts   sts to be increased

Stitches to be increased divided by 2 is the number of stitches to be increased per side.

$$\underline{\hspace{2cm}} \div 2 = \underline{\hspace{2.5cm}}$$
sts   sts increased per side

Number of increase stitches per side minus 1 gives the number of increase increments.

$$\underline{\hspace{2cm}} - 1 = \underline{\hspace{2.5cm}}$$
sts   increase increments

Divide the rows available for increases (as previously calculated) by the number of increase increments. This gives the number of rows between increases. Remember to round off—no half rows.

$$\underline{\hspace{1.5cm}} \div \underline{\hspace{1.5cm}} = \underline{\hspace{2.5cm}}$$
rows   increments   rows between increases

The number of rows between increases may be adjusted for best fit.

Inc 1 st each side every _____ row _____ times. Then every _____ row _____ times.

Inc 1 st each side every RS row 2 (6, 26, 32, 40) times. Then, every 4th row 20 (18, 8, 5, 1) time(s).

Continue in St st until piece measures _____ inches from beg.

Continue in St st until piece measures 17½ inches from beg.

Sleeve cap shaping
The number of initial armhole bind-off stitches for the sleeve and the body of the garment should match. These parts will need to match up when seaming together.
  Bind off the same number of stitches indicated for the back of the sweater at the armhole bind-off. Then, mirror the decreases indicated at the back armhole.

Bind off _____ sts at beg of next 2 rows. Bind off _____ sts at beg of following 2 rows (match front/back).

Bind off 4 (5, 7, 8, 9) sts at the beg of the next 2 rows. Bind off 4 (5, 6, 7, 8) sts at the beg of the following 2 rows.

In this pattern, the sleeve cap is the same length from underarm bind-offs to the top as the armhole opening is on the sweater.

Example: 8 inches from underarm bind-off on sweater to shoulder shaping. Sleeve cap should be 8 inches from underarm bind-off to top of the sleeve cap. Because this is a knitted piece, the sleeve may be "eased" into the armhole when seaming. It's important to make sure the length along the bound-off edge is the same length as the shaped armhole edge. Be careful to prevent puckering.

Using the number of rows per inch from the gauge swatch, calculate the number of rows needed for the sleeve cap.

Example: 8-inch sleeve cap times 7 rows per inch = 56 rows. This is the total number of rows needed for the sleeve to fit properly into the armhole opening.

Sleeve cap length times gauge = the number of rows needed for the cap.

$$\underline{\qquad}'' \times \underline{\qquad} = \underline{\qquad\qquad}$$
inches   rows   rows for cap

Subtract the number of rows used in the underarm bind-offs above. The remaining number is the rows needed to complete the sleeve cap.

Rows for sleeve cap minus rows used in the bottom armhole decreases = the rows remaining to complete the sleeve cap.

$$\underline{\qquad\qquad} - \underline{\qquad\qquad} = \underline{\qquad\qquad}$$
rows for cap   rows used   rows remaining for cap completion

There should be 3 inches flat area at the top of the sleeve cap. This matches the shoulder area of the armhole opening. In our example, 3 times 5 = 15 stitches for the flat area at the top.

3 inches times stitch gauge = the number of stitches at the shoulder edge (top of sleeve cap).

$$3'' \times \underline{\qquad} = \underline{\qquad\qquad}$$
sts   sts at top of cap

Stitches at the top of the cap plus 16 for shaping = total sts used at sleeve top.

$$\underline{\qquad} + 16\ sts = \underline{\qquad\qquad}$$
sts   sts at top of sleeve

Determine the number of stitches remaining on the sleeve after the underarm bind-offs. Subtract the stitches needed for the shaping at the top of the sleeve cap. Divide the remaining number in 2 for the mirrored decreases on each side of the sleeve cap. If the number is not an even number, adjust the stitch count in the flat area.

$$(\underline{\qquad\qquad} - \underline{\qquad\qquad}) \div 2 = \underline{\qquad\qquad}$$
sts remaining   sts at top of cap   sts to be decreased at each side of the sleeve cap

Evenly space the decrease stitches along the remaining rows needed to complete the sleeve, work extra stitches in at the bottom of the sleeve cap.

Dec 1 st each side every RS row _____ times.

Then dec 1 st each side, every row _____ times.

Bind off _____ sts at beg of next 4 rows.

Bind off rem _____ sts.

Dec 1 st each side every RS row 8 (10, 12, 14, 17) times. Then dec 1 st each side every RS row 18 (16, 14, 12, 8) times. Bind off 3 (3, 4, 4, 4) sts at the beg of the next 4 rows. Bind off rem 16 (22, 36, 42, 50) sts.

Finishing

Question: To block or not to block?

Answer: BLOCK!

Blocking is just as important as knitting. Blocking permits exact matching of stitches and seams. It also provides the opportunity to slightly reshape the finished pieces if needed.

Use this opportunity to determine buttonhole placement (if desired). Use locking-stitch markers or coil-less safety pins to mark the buttonhole locations along the right front. The bottom buttonhole should be ½ inch from the lower edge of the piece. Because the right front does not have the neckband yet, the top buttonhole should be approximately ½ inch down from the top of the neckband. The neckband will have the final buttonhole placed 2 rows below the top of the neckband.

Determine how large the buttons are, and how many you want on the cardigan. Using a tape measure or yardstick, evenly space the buttonholes between the top and bottom buttonholes previously marked.

Note: To avoid gaps, we recommend a button be placed at the bustline, hips and waist. Space other buttons evenly in between.

A slightly easier option for using buttons on the cardigan is to use them as decoration, without buttonholes. Work up the right front band the same as the left front band. After the cardigan is sewn together, simply place decorative buttons evenly spaced along the left front band.

Make sample buttonhole to ensure button fits:

1. Cast on 10 stitches, work knit 1, purl 1 rib for two rows.

2. Measure the button width on the sample and convert it to stitches.

3. On Row 3, work in pattern to first stitch of buttonhole. Bind off the number of stitches required to fit the button. Work balance of row.

4. On Row 4, work in pattern, casting on stitches above the bound-off stitches in Row 3. Complete row.

5. Work 2 more rows in rib pattern.

6. Bind off in pattern.

7. Determine that button slips through hole snugly. Adjust number of buttonhole stitches if needed.

Block all pieces. Mark buttonholes along right front center edge. Sew shoulder seams.

Front bands & neckband

Attaching front bands to the cardigan requires picking up stitches along rows. Knitted stitches are slightly "fatter" than they are "tall." Because of this, the number of rows is approximately 25 percent more than the number of stitches in an inch.

For the finished bands to lay flat against the garment pieces, pick up and knit 3 stitches out of 4 rows along the front. Pick up and knit every stitch along a horizontal section.

Front bands

With RS facing, using smaller needles, pick up and knit 3 for every 4 rows along center front. Work in k1, p1 rib for 1½ inches, working buttonholes on 4th row along right front band. Bind off loosely in rib.

Neckband

With RS facing, using smaller needles, beg at center front neck edge, pick up and knit stitches from top edge of right front band; pick up and knit neck bound-off sts; pick up and knit 3 sts for every 4 rows along the side neck edge; pick up and knit back neck sts; pick up and knit 3 sts for every 4 rows along the side neck edge; pick up and knit neckline bound-off sts; pick up and knit sts along top of left front band. Work in k1, p1 rib for 1 inch, working buttonhole at beg of 4th row, 2 sts from right front edge. Bind off loosely in rib.

Sew sleeves into armholes. Sew sleeve and side seams, matching seams at underarm. Weave in all tails. Lightly reblock finished garment if necessary. Sew buttons onto to button band to correspond to buttonholes. ●

Simply Fitting Shell

A basic shell becomes so much more when the fit is perfect and the color makes you feel wonderful.

Design by Kristin Hansen

. . . .

Skill Level
 EASY

Sizes
Woman's 1X-large (2X-large, 3X-large, 4X-large, 5X-large) Instructions are given for smallest size, with larger sizes in parentheses. When only 1 number is given, it applies to all sizes.

Finished Measurement
Chest: 46 (50, 54, 58, 62) inches

Materials
- Conjoined Creations Dance Party (worsted weight; 100% soysilk; 125 yds/60g per skein): 7 (8, 10, 11, 12) skeins frug
- Size 7 (4.5mm) straight and 16-inch circular needles
- Size 8 (5mm) needles or size needed to obtain gauge
- Stitch markers
- Stitch holders

Gauge
20 sts and 24 rows = 4 inches/10cm St st on larger needles.

To save time, take time to check gauge.

Special Abbreviation
Knit in front and back (kfb): Inc 1 st by knitting in front and back of next st.

Pattern Stitch
K1, P1 Rib (odd number of sts in rows)
Row 1 (RS): K1, *p1, k1; rep from * across.
Row 2: P1, *k1, p1; rep from * across.
Rep Rows 1 and 2 for pat.

K1, P1 Rib (even number of sts in rnds)
Rnd 1: *K1, p1; rep from * around.
Rep Rnd 1 for pat.

Pattern Notes
Shell is designed with a positive ease of 1–2 inches for a close fit.

Work increases and decreases 1 stitch in from the edge. When decreasing, work a slip, slip, knit (ssk) decrease at the beginning of the row and a knit 2 together (k2tog) decrease at the end of the row.

Back

Ribbing
With smaller needles, cast on 103 (111, 121, 129, 139) sts.

Work in K1, P1 Rib pat 2½ inches, ending with a RS row.

Next row: Continue in Rib, inc 12 (14, 14, 16, 16) sts evenly across row—115 (125, 135, 145, 155) sts.

Change to larger needles.

Body
Next row (RS): Knit across.

Continue in St st, dec 1 st each side [every 12th row] 3 times—109 (119, 129, 139, 149) sts.

Inc 1 st each side [every 12th row] 3 times—115 (125, 135, 145, 155) sts.

Continue even in St st until back measures 16 (16, 16, 16, 16½) inches from cast-on edge.

Armhole shaping
Bind off [5 (5, 6, 7, 8) sts] at the beg of the next 2 rows, then [4 (5, 6, 7, 8) sts] at the beg of the next 2 rows—97 (105, 111, 117, 123) sts.

Dec 1 st at each side [every RS row] 8 (10, 11, 13, 15) times—81 (85, 89, 91, 93) sts.

Continue in St st until armhole measures 8 (9, 9½, 10, 10½) inches.

Shape shoulders

Bind off [7 (7, 8, 8, 8) sts] at the beg of the next 2 rows, [7 (7, 8, 8, 8) sts] at the beg of the next 2 rows, then [7 (8, 8, 8, 8) sts] at the beg of the next 2 rows—39 (41, 41, 43, 45) sts.

Place rem sts on holder.

Front

Work same as for back to armhole shaping.

Armhole & neck shaping

Bind off [5 (5, 6, 7, 8) sts] at the beg of the next 2 rows, then [4 (5, 6, 7, 8) sts] at the beg of the next 2 rows—97 (105, 111, 117, 123) sts.

Dec 1 st at each side [every RS row] 8 (10, 11, 13, 15) times. *At the same time,* when armhole measures 4 inches, on next RS row, work to center 13 (13, 13, 15, 15) sts, place center 13 (13, 13, 15, 15) sts on st holder; join 2nd ball of yarn and work to end of row.

Working both sides at once with separate yarn, bind off 2 sts at each neck edge 3 times, then dec 1 st at each neck edge [every RS row] 7 (8, 8, 8, 9) times—21 (22, 24, 24, 24) sts each side.

Continue in St st until armhole measures 8 (9, 9½, 10, 10½) inches.

Shape shoulders

Bind off at each shoulder [7 (7, 8, 8, 8) sts] twice, [7 (7, 8, 8, 8) sts] twice, then [7 (8, 8, 8, 8) sts] once.

Finishing

Block back and front. Sew shoulder and side seams.

Neckband

With smaller circular needle, beg at left shoulder seam, pick up and knit 3 sts for every 4 rows along left neckline, knit sts from front neck holder, pick up and knit 3 sts for every 4 rows along right neckline, knit sts from back neck holder, adjusting sts if necessary to have an even number. Place marker for beg of rnd and join.

Work in K1, P1 Rib pat for 1 inch.

Bind off loosely in pat.

Armhole band

With smaller circular needle, beg at underarm seam, pick up and knit in underarm bound-off sts, pick up and knit 3 sts for every 4 rows around armhole, pick up and knit rem bound-off sts. Place marker for beg of rnd and join.

Work in K1, P1 Rib pat for 1 inch.

Bind off loosely in pat.

Weave in ends and lightly reblock if necessary. •

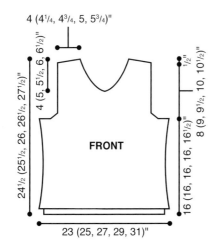

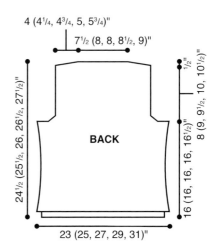

Simply Fitting Cardigan

Every woman needs a basic sweater in her wardrobe. Make this in a color you love to wear!

Design by Kristin Hansen

Skill Level

◼◼◻◻ EASY

Sizes

Woman's 1X-large (2X-large, 3X-large, 4X-large, 5X-large) Instructions are given for smallest size, with larger sizes in parentheses. When only 1 number is given, it applies to all sizes.

Finished Measurement

Chest: 48 (52, 56, 60, 64) inches

Materials

- Conjoined Creations Dance Party (worsted weight; 100% soysilk; 125 yds/60g per skein): 12 (13, 16, 17, 19) skeins stroll
- Size 7 (4.5mm) straight and 16-inch circular needles
- Size 8 (5mm) needles or size needed to obtain gauge
- Stitch markers
- Stitch holders
- 6 (1-inch) buttons

Gauge

20 sts and 24 rows = 4 inches/10cm in St st on larger needles.

To save time, take time to check gauge.

Pattern Stitch

K1, P1 Rib (odd number of sts in rows)
Row 1 (RS): K1, *p1, k1; rep from * across.
Row 2: P1, *k1, p1; rep from * across.
Rep Rows 1 and 2 for pat.

K1, P1 Rib (even number of sts in rnds)
Rnd 1: *K1, p1; rep from * around.
Rep Rnd 1 for pat.

Pattern Notes

Work decreases 1 stitch in from edge.

Work a slip, slip, knit (ssk) decrease at the beginning of the row and a knit 2 together (k2tog) decrease at the end of the row.

Back

With larger needles, cast on 132 (143, 154, 165, 176) sts.

Work in K1, P1 Rib until piece measures 2½ inches, ending with a RS row.

Next row (WS): Work in rib, dec 12 (13, 14, 15, 16) sts evenly spaced across—120 (130, 140, 150, 160) sts.

Work in St st until back measures 16 (16, 16, 16, 16½) inches from cast-on edge, ending with a WS row.

Armhole shaping

Bind off [4 (5, 7, 8, 9) sts] at the beg of the next 2 rows, then [4 (5, 6, 7, 8) sts] at the beg of the next 2 rows—104 (110, 114, 120, 126) sts.

Dec 1 st at each side [every RS row] 8 (10, 12, 14, 17) times—88 (90, 90, 92, 92) sts.

Continue in St st until armhole measures 8½ (9, 9½, 10, 10½) inches.

Shape shoulders

Bind off [8 (8, 8, 8, 7) sts] at the beg of the next 2 rows, [8 (8, 8, 8, 8) sts] at the beg of the next 2 rows, and then [9 (9, 9, 9, 8) sts] the beg of the next 2 rows—38 (40, 40, 42, 46) sts.

Place sts on holder.

Right Front

With larger needles, cast on 66 (71, 77, 82, 88) sts. Work in K1, P1 Rib until piece measures 2½ inches, ending with a RS row.

Next row (WS): Work in rib pat, dec 6 (6, 7, 7, 8) sts evenly spaced across—60 (65, 70, 75, 80) sts.

Work in St st until front measures 16 (16, 16, 16, 16½) inches from cast-on edge, ending with a RS row.

Armhole shaping

Bind off at armhole edge [4 (5, 7, 8, 9) sts] once, then [4 (5, 6, 7, 8) sts] once—52 (55, 57, 60, 63) sts.

Dec 1 st at armhole edge [every RS row] 8 (10, 12, 14, 17) times—44 (45, 45, 46, 46) sts.

Continue in St st until armhole measures 6 (6½, 6, 6, 6½) inches, ending with a WS row.

Neck shaping

Bind off 12 (13, 10, 11, 12) sts at beg of next RS row. Dec 1 st at neck edge [every RS row] 7 (7, 10, 10, 11) times—25 (25, 26, 25, 23) sts.

Continue in St st, if necessary, until armhole measures 8½ (9, 9½, 10, 10½) inches, ending with a RS row.

Shape shoulders

Bind off at armhole edge [8 (8, 8, 8, 7) sts] once, [8 (8, 8, 8, 8) sts] once, then rem 9 (9, 9, 9, 8) sts.

Left Front

With larger needles, cast on 66 (71, 77, 82, 88). Work in K1, P1 Rib for 2½ inches, ending with a RS row.

Next row (WS): Dec 6 (6, 7, 7, 8) sts evenly spaced across row—60 (65, 70, 75, 80) sts.

Work in St st until front measures 16 (16, 16, 16, 16½) inches from cast-on edge, ending with a WS row.

Armhole shaping

Bind off at armhole edge [4 (5, 7, 8, 9) sts] once, then [4 (5, 6, 7, 8) sts] once—52 (55, 57, 60, 63) sts.

Dec 1 st at armhole edge, [every RS row] 8 (10, 12, 14, 17) times—44 (45, 45, 46, 46) sts.

Continue in St st until armhole measures 6 (6½, 6, 6, 6½) inches, ending with a RS row.

Neck shaping

Bind off 12 (13, 10, 11, 12) sts at beg of next WS row. Dec 1 st at neck edge [every RS row] 7 (7, 10, 10, 11) times—25 (25, 26, 25, 23) sts.

Continue in St st, if necessary, until armhole measures 8½ (9, 9½, 10, 10½) inches, ending with a WS row.

Shape shoulders

Bind off at armhole edge [8 (8, 8, 8, 7) sts] once, [8 (8, 8, 8, 8) sts] once, and then rem 9 (9, 9, 9, 8) sts.

Sleeve

With smaller needles, cast on 47 (51, 55, 59, 61) sts. Work in K1, P1 Rib for 2½ inches, ending with a RS row.

Next row (WS): Working in rib, inc 5 (7, 7, 7, 7) sts evenly spaced across row—52 (58, 62, 66, 68) sts.

Change to larger needles.

Work in St st, inc 1 st each side [every RS row] 2 (6, 26, 32, 40) times, then [every 4th row] 20 (18, 8, 5, 1) times—96 (106, 130, 140, 150) sts.

Continue in St st until sleeve measures 17½ inches from cast-on edge.

Cap shaping

Bind off [4 (5, 7, 8, 9) sts] at the beg of the next 2 rows, and then 4 (5, 6, 7, 8) sts] at the beg of the next 2 rows—80 (86, 104, 110, 116) sts.

Dec 1 st each side [every RS row] 8 (10, 12, 14, 17) times, then [every row] 18 (16, 14, 12, 8) times—28 (34, 52, 58, 66) sts.

Bind off [3 (4, 5, 5, 6) sts] at the beg of the next 4 rows—16 (18, 32, 38, 42) sts.

Bind off all sts.

Finishing

Block all pieces. Sew shoulder seams.

Left front band

With RS facing and smaller needles, pick up and knit 3 sts for every 4 rows along center front.

Work in K1, P1 Rib for 1½ inches. Bind off loosely in rib.

Place markers for 5 buttons evenly spaced along left front band. Rem buttonhole is worked in neck-band ribbing.

Right front band

With RS facing and smaller needles, pick up and knit 3 sts for every 4 rows along center front.

Work 3 rows in K1, P1 Rib.

Next row (buttonhole row): Work in rib to first marker, bind off 2 sts, *work in rib to next marker, bind off 2 sts; rep from * 4 times, rib to end of row.

Next row: Work in rib across, casting on 2 sts over the bound-off sts from the previous row.

Continue in rib pat until ribbing measures 1½ inches. Bind off loosely in rib.

Neckband

With RS facing and smaller needles, beg at center front neck edge, pick up and knit sts from top edge of front band; pick up and knit neck bound-off st; 3 sts for every 4 rows along front neck edge; in each st across back neck sts; 3 sts for every 4 rows along front neck edge; and in each bound-off st at neck; pick up and knit sts from top edge of front band.

Work 3 rows in K1, P1 Rib.

Next row (buttonhole row): Work 2 sts in rib, bind off 2 sts, rib to end of row.

Next row: Work in rib across, casting on 2 sts over the bound-off sts on previous row.

Next row: Work in rib across.

Bind off loosely in rib.

Sew in sleeves. Sew sleeve and side seams. Sew buttons opposite buttonholes.

Lightly reblock finished garment if necessary. ●

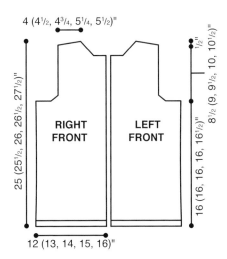

4 (4½, 4¾, 5¼, 5½)"

RIGHT FRONT

LEFT FRONT

25 (25½, 26, 26½, 27½)"

½"

8½ (9, 9½, 10, 10½)"

16 (16, 16, 16½)"

12 (13, 14, 15, 16)"

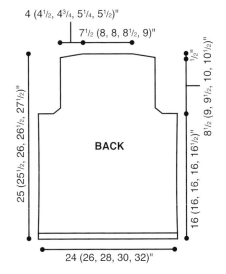

4 (4½, 4¾, 5¼, 5½)"

7½ (8, 8, 8½, 9)"

½"

BACK

25 (25½, 26, 26½, 27½)"

8½ (9, 9½, 10, 10½)"

16 (16, 16, 16, 16½)"

24 (26, 28, 30, 32)"

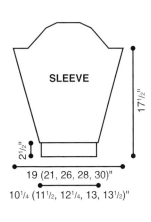

SLEEVE

17½"

2½"

19 (21, 26, 28, 30)"

10¼ (11½, 12¼, 13, 13½)"

Skipping Stones

This casual jacket has a bit of patterning, plus a contrasting trim, to place the accent where you want it.

Design by Kate Lemmers

. . . .

Skill Level

■■■□ INTERMEDIATE

Size

Woman's 1X-large (2X-large, 3X-large, 4X-large, 5X-large) Instructions are given for smallest size, with larger sizes in parentheses. When only 1 number is given, it applies to all sizes.

Finished Measurements

Chest: 46 (51, 52½, 58, 64) inches (including trim)
Length: 30 (31, 32, 33, 34) inches

Materials

- Kraemer Yarns Tatamy Tweed (DK weight; 55% acrylic/45% cotton; 250 yds/100g per skein): 8 (10, 10, 12, 13) skeins merlot (MC) and 1 (1, 1, 1, 2) skein(s) birch tweed (CC)
- Size 7 (4.5mm) 36-inch and 47-inch or longer circular needles (for collar) or size needed to obtain gauge; 47–60-inch circular needle for trim
- Stitch holders

Gauge

20 sts and 23½ rows = 4 inches/10cm in Checkered Dash pat (after blocking).

To save time, take time to check gauge.

Pattern Stitch

Checkered Dash (multiple of 8 sts + 8)
Row 1 (RS): K1, *k6, p2; rep from * to last 7 sts, k7.
Row 2: P7, *k2, p6; rep from * to last st, p1.
Rows 3–10: Rep [Rows 1 and 2] 4 times.
Row 11: K1, *k2, p2, k4; rep from * to last 7 sts, k2, p2, k3.

Row 12: P3, k2, p2, *p4, k2, p2; rep from * to last st, p1.
Rows 13–20: Rep [Rows 11 and 12] 4 times.
Rep Rows 1–20 for pat.
Note: A chart is included for those preferring to work pat st from a chart.

Special Technique

3-needle bind-off: Hold sections of garment with RS tog, the tips of the 2 needles should be facing in the same direction. Using a 3rd needle, *insert needle into first st on front needle and then first st on back needle and knit these 2 sts tog; rep from * once more and pass first st on RH needle over 2nd st on RH needle. Continue in same manner until all sts are worked tog. Pull yarn through last st.

Pattern Notes

A circular needle is used to accommodate stitches. Do not join; work back and forth in rows.

For ease of picking up stitches and seaming, work all increases and decreases 1 stitch in from the edge.

Back

With MC, cast on 120 (128, 136, 144, 160) sts.

Knit 4 rows.

Work Checkered Dash pat until back measures 21 (21, 21½, 22, 22) inches from cast-on edge, ending with a WS row.

Armhole shaping

Bind off 8 (8, 11, 12, 16) sts at beg of the next 2 rows—104 (112, 114, 120, 128) sts.

Dec 1 st at each side [every RS row] 8 (8, 9, 8, 12) times—88 (96, 96, 104, 104) sts.

Continue in established pat until back measures 30 (31, 32, 33, 34) inches from cast-on edge, ending with a WS row.

Next row (RS): Work in pat over 24 (27, 25, 28, 27) sts, join 2nd skein of MC and bind off 40 (42, 46, 48 50) sts, work rem sts in pat. Place sts on holders.

Right Front
With MC, cast on 56 (64, 64, 72, 80) sts.

Knit 4 rows.

Work in Checkered Dash pat until front measures 21 (21, 21½, 22, 22) inches from cast-on edge, ending with a WS row.

Neck & armhole shaping
Dec 1 st by k2tog at neck edge [every RS row] 8 (15, 9, 18, 18) times, and then [every other RS row] 8 (6, 10, 6, 7) times. *At the same time,* bind off at armhole edge 8 (8, 11, 12, 16) sts once, then dec 1 st by ssk at armhole edge [every RS row] 8 (8, 9, 8, 12) times—24 (27, 25, 28, 27) sts.

Continue even in established pat until front measures 30 (31, 32, 33, 34) inches from cast-on edge, ending with a RS row.

Place sts on holder.

Left Front
With MC, cast on 56 (64, 64, 72, 80) sts.

Knit 4 rows.

Work in Checkered Dash pat until front measures 21 (21, 21½, 22, 22) inches from cast-on edge, ending with a WS row.

Neck & armhole shaping
Bind off at armhole edge 8 (8, 11, 12, 16) sts once, and then dec 1 by k2tog [every RS row] 8 (8, 9, 8, 12) times. *At the same time,* dec 1 st by ssk at neck edge [every RS row] 8 (15, 9, 18, 18) times and then [every other RS row] 8 (6, 10, 6, 7) times—24 (27, 25, 28, 27) sts.

Continue even in established pat until front measures 30 (31, 32, 33, 34) inches from cast-on edge, ending with a RS row.

Place sts on holder.

Sleeves
With MC, cast on 48 (56, 56, 64, 72) sts.

Knit 4 rows.

Beg Checkered Dash pat inc 1 st at each side [every 4th row] 0 (0, 11, 13, 13) times, [every 6th row] 2 (4, 9, 7, 7) times, and then [every 8th row] 10 (10, 0, 0, 0) times, working inc sts into pat—72 (84, 96, 104, 112) sts.

Work even in pat until sleeve measures 17½ (18, 18, 18½, 18½) inches from cast-on edge, ending with a WS row.

Bind off 8 (8, 11, 12, 16) sts at beg of next 2 rows—56 (68, 74, 80, 80) sts.

Dec 1 st at each side [every RS row] 8 (8, 9, 8, 12) times—40 (52, 56, 64, 56) sts.

Work even in pat for 9 (9, 7, 11, 17) rows, ending with a WS row.

Cap shaping

Dec 1 st at each side [every RS row] 6 (9, 11, 11, 7) times.

Bind off 0 (2, 0, 5, 3) sts at the beg of the next 2 rows, then 4 (5, 7, 6, 8) at the beg of the next 2 rows—20 sts.

Bind off rem sts.

Finishing

Block pieces.

Join shoulders seams using 3-needle bind-off.

Trim

With RS facing, longer circular needle and CC, and beg at lower right front, pick up and knit 83 (83, 84, 87, 87) sts along right front, pick up and knit 40 (42, 46, 48, 50) sts across back neck and 83 (83, 84, 87, 87) sts along left front—206 (208, 214, 222, 224) sts.

Beg with WS row, work 8 rows in St st.

Bind off loosely.

Cuffs

With RS of sleeve facing and CC, skipping first and last st, pick up and knit 46 (54, 54, 62, 70) sts along cast-on edge.

Next row: Purl across.

Next row: Knit across, inc 4 sts evenly spaced—50 (58, 58, 66, 74) sts.

Work 6 rows in St st.

Bind off loosely.

Sew sleeves to front and back centering top of sleeve at shoulder seam. Sew sleeve and side seams beg at lower edge and working toward cuff.

Weave in all ends. ●

STITCH KEY
☐ K on RS, p on WS
⊟ P on RS, k on WS

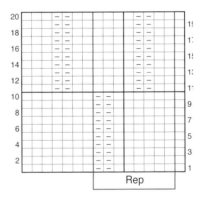

Checkered Dash Chart

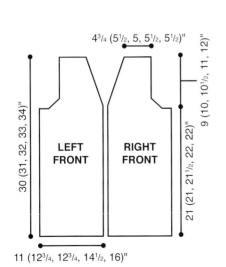

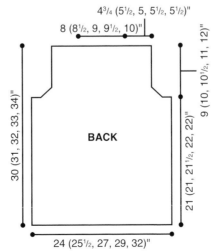

Make Me Blush

Big girls like to show off their curves, too! This pullover features unusual waist shaping and dramatic patterned cuffs.

Design by Amy Polcyn

Skill Level
■■□□ EASY

Sizes
Woman's 1X-large (2X-large, 3X-large, 4X-large, 5X-large) Instructions are given for smallest size, with larger sizes in parentheses. When only 1 number is given, it applies to all sizes.

Finished Measurements
Chest: 42½ (47, 50½, 55, 58½) inches
Length: 25½ (26, 27, 27½, 28½) inches

Materials
- Berroco Lustra (worsted weight; 50% Peruvian wool/50% tencel; 197 yds/100g per hank): 5 (6, 6, 7, 7) hanks burgundy #3155
- Size 8 (5mm) 24-inch circular needle or size needed to obtain gauge
- Locking stitch markers

[4 MEDIUM]

Gauge
18 sts and 22 rows = 4 inches/10cm in St st (blocked).

18 sts and 25 rows = 4 inches/10cm in Lace pat (blocked).

To save time, take time to check gauge.

Special Abbreviations
Make 1 Left (M1L): Insert LH needle from front to back under horizontal strand between last st worked and next st on LH needle, k1-tbl.

Make 1 Right (M1R): Insert LH needle from back to front under horizontal strand between last st worked and next st on LH needle, k1 through front of loop.

Centered Double Decrease (CDD): Slip next 2 sts as if to k2tog, k1, p2sso.

Pattern Stitch
Lace Pattern (see chart)

Pattern Note
Locking stitch markers are used to mark the center stitch of each centered double decrease and increase for the princess seam lines. Move the markers up as you work.

Back
Cast on 96 (106, 114, 124, 132) sts.

Knit 3 rows, ending with a WS row.

Work in St st until piece measures 5 (5, 5½, 5½, 6) inches, ending with a WS row.

Place markers on 25th (27th, 29th, 31st, 33rd) st from each end.

Waist shaping
Row 1 (RS): *Knit to 1 st before marked st, CDD; rep from * once more, then knit to end—92 (102, 110, 120, 128) sts.

Rows 2 and 4: Purl across.

Row 3: *Knit to marked st, sl 1; rep from * once more, then knit to end of row.

Rows 5–16: Rep [Rows 1–4] 3 more times—80 (90, 98, 108, 116) sts.

Rows 17 and 18: Rep Rows 3 and 4.

Row 19 (RS): *Knit to marked st, M1L, knit to marked st, M1R; rep from * once more, then knit to end of row—84 (94, 102, 112, 120) sts.

Rows 20 and 22: Purl across.

Row 21: *Knit to marked st, sl 1; rep from * once more, then knit to end of row.

Rep [Rows 19–22] twice more, then [Rows 19 and 20] once more—96 (106, 114, 124, 132) sts.

Continue even in St st until back measures 16 (16½, 17, 17½, 18) inches from cast-on edge, ending with a WS row.

Armhole shaping
Bind off 6 (8, 9, 10, 12) sts at the beg of the next 2 rows—84 (90, 96, 104, 108) sts.

Dec 1 st at each side [every RS row] 5 (7, 9, 11, 12) times—74 (76, 78, 82, 84) sts.

Continue even in St st until armhole measures 7½ (7½, 8, 8, 8½) inches, ending with a WS row.

Neck shaping
Mark center 22 (22, 24, 24, 26) sts.

Knit to marker; join 2nd ball of yarn and bind off center 22 (22, 24, 24, 26) sts; knit to end of row—26 (27, 27, 29, 29) sts each side.

Working both sides at once with separate yarn, dec 1 st each neck edge [every RS row] twice, ending with a WS row—24 (25, 25, 27, 27) sts each side.

Shape shoulders
Bind off at each shoulder [8 (9, 9, 9, 9) sts] once, then [8 (8, 8, 9, 9) sts] twice.

Front
Work same as for back until front measures 14½ (15, 15½, 16, 16½) inches from cast-on edge.

Neck shaping
Mark center 12 (12, 12, 12, 14) sts.

Knit to marker; join 2nd ball of yarn and bind off center 12 (12, 12, 12, 14) sts; knit to end of row.

Working both sides at once with separate yarn, dec 1 st each neck edge [every 6 rows] 7 (7, 8, 8, 8) times. *At the same time*, when front measures 16 (16½, 17, 17½, 18) inches from cast-on edge, on next RS row, shape armholes same as for back—24 (25, 25, 27, 27) sts rem for each side.

Continue even in St st until armhole measures 8½ (8½, 9, 9, 9½) inches, ending with a WS row.

Shape shoulders
Bind off at each shoulder [8 (9, 9, 9, 9) sts] once, then [8 (8, 8, 9, 9) sts] twice.

Sleeve
Cast on 64 sts.

Knit 4 rows, ending with a RS row.

Work [Rows 1–8 of Lace pat] 5 times (sleeve measures approx 7 inches from cast-on edge).

Work in St st, inc 1 st each side [every 12 (12, 8, 10, 6) rows] 2 (4, 6, 2, 4) times, then [every 10 (0, 0, 8, 8) rows] 2 (0, 0, 4, 4) times—72 (72, 76, 76, 80) sts.

Continue even in St st until piece measures 17 (17½, 18, 18½, 19) inches from cast-on edge, ending with a WS row.

Cap shaping

Bind off 6 (8, 9, 10, 12) sts at the beg of the next 2 rows—60 (56, 58, 56, 56) sts.

Dec 1 st each side [every RS row] 4 (6, 8, 9, 10) times, then [every row] 17 (13, 12, 10, 9) times—18 sts.

Bind off 2 sts at the beg of the next 4 rows—10 sts.

Bind off all sts.

Finishing
Block all pieces. Sew shoulder seams.

Neckband
With RS facing, pick up and knit 132 (132, 136, 136, 142) sts evenly around neck. Place marker for beg of rnd. Join to work in rnds.

Purl 1 rnd. Knit 1 rnd. Purl 1 rnd. Bind off all sts kwise.

Sew in sleeves. Sew sleeve and side seams.

Lightly reblock garment if necessary. •

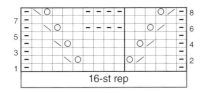

Make Me Blush
Lace Pattern Chart

STITCH KEY
☐ K on RS, p on WS
⊟ P on RS, k on WS
⊙ Yo
⟋ K2tog on RS
⟍ Ssk on RS

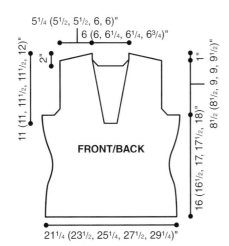

FRONT/BACK

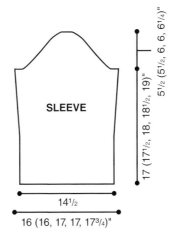

SLEEVE

Dappled Shadows

Subtle blending of three shades of yarn with a delicate chevron pattern creates a vest for all seasons.

Design by Michael del Vecchio

Skill Level
■■■□ INTERMEDIATE

Sizes
Woman's 1X-large (2X-large, 3X-large, 4X-large, 5X-large) Instructions are given for smallest size, with larger sizes in parentheses. When only 1 number is given, it applies to all sizes.

Finished Measurements
Chest: 46½ (51, 55½, 60, 64½) inches
Length: 22 (22½, 23, 23½, 24) inches

Materials
- Fibra Natura Exquisite Bamboo (worsted weight; 77% bamboo/ 23% superwash merino; 109 yds/50g per skein): 4 (4, 5, 5, 6) skeins chocolate #40669 (A), 5 (5, 6, 6, 7) skeins sable #40156 (B), 3 (3, 3, 4, 4) skeins tawny birch #40154 (C)
- Size 7 (4.5mm) 24-inch circular and double-point needles (for I-cord trim) or size needed to obtain gauge
- 3 (1-inch) buttons from JHB #70258
- Stitch holders
- Stitch markers

4 MEDIUM

Gauge
20 sts and 24 rows = 4 inches/10cm in St st.

1 rep Lace & Chevron pat = 2¼ inches, blocked.

To save time, take time to check gauge.

Special Abbreviation
Slip, knit 2 together, pass slip stitch over (sk2p):
Slip the next st, k2tog, then pass the slipped st over the st resulting from the k2tog to dec 2 sts.

Pattern Stitches
Lace & Chevron (multiple of 14 sts + 1)
Row 1 (RS): *K1, yo, k5, sk2p, k5, yo; rep from * to last st, end k1.
Row 2: Purl across.
Rep Rows 1 and 2 for pat.

Stripe Sequence
*4 rows A,
4 rows B,
4 rows C,
4 rows B; rep from * for pat.

Special Technique
3-needle bind-off: Hold sections of garment with RS tog, the tips of the 2 needles should be facing in the same direction. Using a 3rd needle, *insert needle into first st on front needle and then first st on back needle and knit these 2 sts tog; rep from * once more and pass first st on RH needle over 2nd st on RH needle. Continue in same manner until all sts are worked tog. Pull yarn through last st.

Pattern Notes
All measurements are blocked measurements. Work a substantial gauge swatch, and then block to determine exact measurements.

The Lace & Chevron pattern is repeated throughout garment in the Stripe Sequence indicated.

Body of vest is worked in 1 piece to armhole and then divided for back and fronts.

When working armhole and neck shaping, work any partial pattern repeats in stockinette stitch.

Bind off armhole and neck edge stitches very loosely or with a larger needle.

An applied I-cord edging is worked on armholes, neck and front edges for stability and style. After the first few rows of the edging are worked, test the stretch and durability of the I-cord, which should be

snug but should not cause edge to buckle. If edging is too tight, change to larger-size needle.

Body
With circular needle and A, cast on 285 (301, 339, 357, 395) sts loosely.

Next row (WS): K2 (3, 1, 3, 1), purl to last 2 (3, 1, 3, 1) st(s), end k2 (3, 1, 3, 1).

Set up pat
Row 1 (RS): K2 (3, 1, 3, 1), work Row 1 of Lace & Chevron pat to last 2 (3, 1, 3, 1) st(s), end k2 (3, 1, 3, 1).

Work 3 rows even in established pat.

Change to B and continue in Lace & Chevron pat and Stripe Sequence until piece measures 13½ inches from cast-on edge, ending with a RS row.

Divide fronts & back
Next row (WS): K2 (3, 1, 3, 1), p56 (56, 68, 68, 80) sts for left front, bind off 28 (28, 32, 32, 36) sts for left armhole, p113 (127, 137, 151, 161) sts for back, bind off 28 (28, 32, 32, 36) sts for right armhole, p56 (56, 68, 68, 80) sts, k2 (3, 1, 3, 1) for right front.

Right Front
Dec row (RS): K2, work in pat to last 3 sts, k2tog, k1—57 (58, 68, 70, 80) sts.

Next row (WS): Work in pat across.

Rep [last 2 rows] 5 (8, 8, 13, 14) more times—52 (50, 60, 57, 66) sts.

Work even in pat until armhole measures 5½ (6, 6½, 7, 7½) inches, ending with a WS row.

Shape neck
Next row (RS): Bind off 23 (23, 27, 25, 29) sts, work in pat across—29 (27, 33, 32, 37) sts.

Next row (WS): Work in pat across.

Dec row (RS): K1, ssk, work in pat across—28 (26, 32, 31, 36) sts.

Rep [last 2 rows] 4 (2, 4, 3, 6) more times—24 (24, 28, 28, 30) sts.

Work even in pat and Stripe Sequence until armhole measures 8½ (9, 9½, 10, 10½) inches, ending with a WS row. Slip rem sts to holder or waste yarn.

Back
With RS facing and continuing in established pat, join yarn for back.

Dec row (RS): K1, ssk, work in pat to last 3 sts, k2tog, k1—111 (125, 135, 149, 159) sts.

Next row: Work in pat across.

Rep [last 2 rows] 5 (8, 8, 13, 14) more times—101 (109, 119, 123, 131) sts.

Work even in pat until armhole measures 8½ (9, 9½, 10, 10½) inches, ending with a WS row.

Work in pat across 24 (24, 28, 28 30) sts and place on holder or waste yarn for shoulder, work in pat across 53 (61, 63, 67, 71) sts and place on holder or waste yarn for back neck, work in pat across rem 24 (24, 28, 28, 30) sts and place on holder or waste yarn.

Left Front
With RS facing and continuing in established pat, join yarn for left front.

Dec row (RS): K1, ssk, work in pat to last 2 sts, k2—57 (58, 68, 70, 80) sts.

Next row (WS): Work in pat across.

Rep [last 2 rows] 5 (8, 8, 13, 14) more times—52 (50, 60, 57, 66) sts.

Work even until armhole measures 5½ (6, 6½, 7, 7½) inches, ending with a RS row.

Shape neck
Next row (WS): Bind off 23 (23, 27, 25, 29) sts, work in pat to end of row—29 (27, 33, 32, 37) sts.

Dec row (RS): Work in pat to last 3 sts, k2tog, k1—28 (26, 32, 31, 36) sts.

Next row: Work in pat across.

Rep [last 2 rows] 4 (2, 4, 3, 6) more times—24 (24, 28, 28, 30) sts.

Work even in pat and Stripe Sequence until armhole measures 8½ (9, 9½, 10, 10½) inches, ending with a WS row. Slip rem sts to holder or waste yarn.

Finishing
With A, join shoulders using 3-needle bind-off, working from armhole edge to neck edge.

Neck border
With RS facing and circular needle, beg at right front neck edge, pick up and knit 35 (35, 39, 37, 41) sts to right shoulder seam, knit across 53 (61, 63, 67, 71) sts on waste yarn across back neck, and pick up and knit 35 (35, 39, 37, 41) sts to left front neck edge—123 (131, 141, 141, 153) sts.

Knit 3 rows.

Slip sts to waste yarn.

Front & neck I-cord edging
Mark placement of buttonholes along right front edge, having first at neck edge and rem 2 placed 3 inches apart.

With A and dpns, cast on 3 sts. Beg at lower right front edge and working attached I-cord as follows: *K2, sl 1 to RH needle, insert tip of RH needle into edge st, sl these sts back to LH needle and k2tog (slipped st and picked-up st), slip all 3 sts back to LH needle, pull yarn across back of work; rep from * to first marker.

I-cord buttonhole: *K3, sl 3 sts back to LH needle without joining I-cord to edge; rep from * 3 times.

Continue with attached I-cord as before skipping approximately 4 edge sts before joining (be sure to check size of buttonhole with button for fit), and working additional buttonholes as marked. Continue around neck edge and along left front edge, working attached I-cord in bound-off sts, in ends of rows at a rate of 3 sts for every 4 rows, and in each "live" st across back of neck around neck edge and along left front to lower edge.

Bind off 3 sts.

Armhole I-cord edging
With A and dpns, cast on 3 sts. Beg at underarm, *k2, sl 1 to RH needle, insert tip of RH needle into edge st at armhole, sl these sts back to LH needle and k2tog (slipped st and picked-up st), slip all 3 sts back to LH needle, pulling yarn across back of work; rep from * joining I-cord to armhole edge at a rate of 3 sts for every 4 rows and in each bound-off st, until I-cord has been applied to entire armhole edge. Bind off 3 sts, leaving a long tail. Sew bound-off edge to cast-on edge of I-cord.

Weave in ends. Sew buttons opposite buttonholes. •

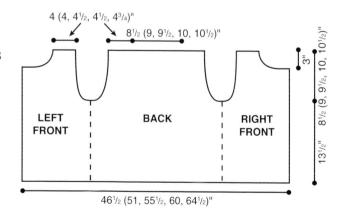

Savoir-Faire

Elegant lines and a dramatic sweep to the neckline create intrigue in this becoming piece.

Design by Kristin Hansen and Sharon Wittenberg

Skill Level
◼◼◼◻ INTERMEDIATE

Sizes
Woman's 1X-large (2X-large, 3X-large, 4X-large, 5X-large) Instructions are given for the smallest size, with larger sizes in parentheses. When only 1 number is given, it applies to all sizes.

Finished Measurements
Chest: 51½ (55½, 60, 64, 69) inches
Length: 31½ inches

Materials
- Conjoined Creations Lyrics Top Ten Collection (worsted weight; 100% silk; 105 yds/50g per skein): 17 (18, 19, 20, 21) skeins suspicious minds
- Size 8 (5mm) 24-inch circular needle or size needed to obtain gauge
- Size 9 (5.5mm) 24-inch circular needle
- Size 10 (6mm) 24-inch circular needle
- Stitch markers
- Stitch holders

4 MEDIUM

Gauge
17 sts and 24 rows = 4 inches/10cm in St st (blocked) on size 8 needles.

To save time, take time to check gauge.

Special Abbreviation
Centered Double Decrease (CDD): Slip next 2 sts as if to k2tog, k1, p2sso.

Pattern Stitch
Seed St (multiple of 2 sts)
Row 1 (RS): *K1, p1; rep from * across.
Row 2: Knit the purl sts and purl the knit sts across.
Rep Row 2 for pat.

Special Technique
3-needle bind-off: Hold sections of garment with RS tog and the tips of the 2 needles should be facing in the same direction. Using a 3rd needle, *insert needle into first st on front needle and then first st on back needle and knit these 2 sts tog; rep from * once more and pass first st on RH needle over 2nd st on RS needle. Continue in same manner until all sts are worked tog. Pull yarn through last st.

Pattern Note
To prevent color pooling, work with two balls of yarn and alternate balls every other row.

Back
With size 8 needle, cast on 115 (124, 133, 142, 151) sts.

Row 1 (RS): K20 (21, 22, 25, 27), yo, CDD, yo, k69 (76, 83, 86, 91), yo, CDD, yo, k20 (21, 22, 25, 27).

Row 2: Purl across.

Rep [Rows 1 and 2] until back measures 11 (11, 11, 10, 10) inches from cast-on edge, ending with a WS row.

Next row (RS): K1, ssk, work in pat to last 3 sts, k2tog, k1—113 (122, 131, 140, 149) sts.

Continue even in pat until back measures 22 (21½, 21½, 20½, 20½) inches from cast-on edge, ending with a WS row.

Next row (RS): K1, ssk, work in pat to last 3 sts, k2tog, k1—111 (120, 129, 138, 147) sts.

Continue even in pat until back measures 23 (22½, 22½, 21½, 21½) inches from cast-on edge, ending with a WS row.

Armhole shaping
Bind off 9 (9, 9, 11, 12) sts at the beg of the next 2 rows—93 (102, 111, 116, 123) sts.

Continue even in established pat until armhole measures 8½ (9, 9, 10, 10) inches, ending with a WS row.

Mark center 37 (38, 37, 40, 41) sts.

Next row (RS): Work in pat over 28 (32, 37, 38, 41) sts; bind off center 37 (38, 37, 40, 41) sts for neck edge, then work in pat over rem sts. Place rem shoulder sts on holders or waste yarn.

Left Front

With size 8 needle, cast on 62 (66, 71, 76, 80) sts.

Row 1 (RS): K20 (21, 22, 25, 27), yo, CDD, yo, knit to last 2 sts, p1, k1.

Row 2: Sl 1p wyif, k1, purl to end of row.

Rep [Rows 1 and 2] until front measures 11 (11, 11, 10, 10) inches from cast-on edge, ending with a WS row.

Next row (RS): K1, ssk, work in pat to end of row—61 (65, 70, 75, 79) sts.

Continue even in pat until front measures 22 (21½, 21½, 20½, 20½) inches from cast-on edge, ending with a WS row.

Next row (RS): K1, ssk, work in pat to end of row—60 (64, 69, 74, 78) sts.

Continue even until front measures 23 (22½, 22½, 21½, 21½) inches from cast-on edge, ending with a WS row.

Armhole shaping

Bind off 9 (9, 9, 11, 12) sts at the beg of the next row—51 (55, 60, 63, 66) sts.

Continue even in established pat until armhole measures 4½ (5, 5, 5½, 5½) inches, ending with a RS row.

Collar

Row 1 (WS): Sl 1p wyif, k1, p1, place marker, work in pat to end of row.

Row 2: Work in pat to marker, work Seed St pat to last 2 sts, p1, k1.

Row 3: Sl 1p wyif, p1, work Seed St pat to marker, remove marker, k1, p1, place marker, work in pat to end of row.

Rep [Rows 2 and 3] 9 (9, 9, 10, 10) more times, moving marker over 2 sts on every RS row, and working these sts in Seed St pat—23 (23, 23, 25, 25) sts at front edge in seed st.

Continue in established pat until armhole measures 8½ (9, 9, 10, 10) inches. Place 23 (23, 23, 25, 25) sts on holder or waste yarn for collar, and rem 28 (32, 37, 38, 41) sts on holder or waste yarn for shoulder.

Right Front

With smallest needle, cast on 62 (66, 71, 76, 80) sts.

Row 1 (RS): Sl 1p wyib, p1, k37 (40, 44, 46, 48), yo, CDD, yo, knit to end of the row.

Row 2: Purl to last 2 sts, k1, p1.

Rep [Rows 1 and 2] until front measures 11 (11, 11, 10, 10) inches from cast-on edge, ending with a WS row.

Next row (RS): Knit across to last 3 sts, k2tog, k1—61 (65, 70, 75, 79) sts.

Continue even in pat until front measures 22 (21½, 21½, 20½, 20½) inches from cast-on edge, ending with a WS row.

Next row (RS): Knit to last 3 sts, k2tog, k1—60 (64, 69, 74, 78) sts.

Continue even in pat until front measures 23 (22½, 22½, 21½, 21½) inches from cast-on edge, ending with a RS row.

Armhole shaping

Bind off 9 (9, 9, 11, 12) sts at the beg of the next row—51 (55, 60, 63, 66) sts.

Continue even in established pat until armhole measures 4½ (5, 5, 5½, 5½) inches, ending with a RS row.

Collar

Row 1 (WS): Work in pat to last 3 sts, place marker, k2, p1.

Row 2: Sl 1p wyib, p1, work Seed St pat to marker, work in pat to end of row.

Row 3: Work in pat to 2 sts before marker, place marker, p1, k1, remove first marker, work in Seed St pat to last 2 sts, k1, p1.

Rep [Rows 2 and 3] 9 (9, 9, 10, 10) more times, moving marker over 2 sts on every RS row, and work these sts in Seed St pat—23 (23, 23, 25, 25) sts at front edge in seed st.

Continue in established pat until armhole measures 8½ (9, 9, 10, 10) inches. Place 23 (23, 23, 25, 25) sts on holder or waste yarn for collar, and rem 28 (32, 37, 38, 41) sts on holder or waste yarn for shoulder.

Sleeve

With size 8 needle, cast on 48 (51, 54, 57, 60) sts.

Row 1 (RS): *K14 (15, 16, 17, 18), yo, CDD, yo; rep from * once more, knit rem 14 (15, 16, 17, 18) sts.

Row 2: Purl across.

Continuing in pat, inc 1 st each side [every 6 rows] 3 (7, 5, 14, 7) times, then [every 8 rows] 10 (7, 8, 1, 6) time(s), working new sts in St st—74 (79, 80, 87, 86) sts.

Continue even in established pat until sleeve measures 17 (17, 16¾, 16¼, 15¾) inches from cast-on edge. Place marker at side edge for underarm.

Continue even in pat until sleeve measures 2 (2, 2, 2½, 2¾) inches from marker, ending with a RS row.

Bind off on next WS row.

Finishing
Block all pieces.

Join shoulder seams using 3-needle bind-off.

Collar
With size 8 needle, and RS facing, work 23 (23, 23, 25, 25) sts of right front in established pat, pick up and

k3 sts on right front to back bound-off sts, pick up and k37 (37, 37, 39, 41) sts along back neck bound-off sts, pick up and k3 sts on left front to holder, work 23 (23, 23, 25, 25) sts of left front in established pat—89 (89, 89, 95, 97) sts.

Next row (WS): Sl 1 wyif, k1, work Seed St pat to last 2 sts, k1, p1.

Work even in established pat for 1 inch.

Change to size 9 needle. Work even in established pat for 1 inch.

Change to size 10 needle. Work even in established pat until collar measures 5 inches from back neck.

Bind off all sts loosely in pat.

Sew sleeves into armholes. Sew side and sleeve seams.

Lightly reblock finished garment if necessary. ●

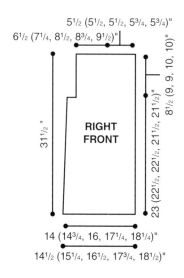

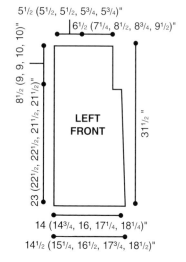

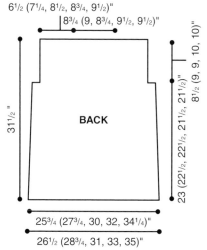

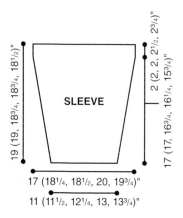

Silken Whispers

This stylish shell coordinates with the Savoir-Faire to create a wear-often twosome.

Design by Sharon Wittenberg

. . . .

Skill Level
■■□□ EASY

Size
Woman's 1X-large (2X-large, 3X-large, 4X-large, 5X-large) Instructions are given for the smallest size, with larger sizes in parentheses. When only 1 number is given, it applies to all sizes.

Finished Measurement
Chest: 47½ (51, 53, 59, 61½) inches

Materials
• Conjoined Creations Lyrics Top Ten Collection (worsted weight; 100% silk; 105 yds/50g per skein): 7 (8, 9, 10, 11) skeins runnin' bare (MC), 1 skein suspicious minds (CC)
• Size 6 (4mm) 32-inch circular needle
• Size 8 (5mm) 32-inch circular needle or size needed to obtain gauge
• Stitch markers

Gauge
18 sts and 26 rows = 4 inches/10cm in St st on larger needle (blocked).

To save time, take time to check gauge.

Pattern Stitch
Seed St (multiple of 2 sts)
Row 1 (RS): *K1, p1; rep from * across.
Row 2: Knit the purl sts and purl the knit sts across.
Rep Row 2 for pat.

Pattern Notes
If making matching Savoir-Faire jacket, it is not necessary to purchase additional yarn in contrasting color for neck trim as there will be sufficient yarn left from the jacket.

There is sufficient yarn to make the entire shell in the main color, if desired.

If using contrasting color for trim, it is necessary to soak this yarn before using it as all hand-dyed yarns have unstable dyes. To prevent "bleeding", it is very important to set the dye with a hot bath of liquid dishwashing detergent followed with a cool bath of fabric softener, water and distilled white vinegar. The natural color of the body of the shell is undyed.

Circular needle is used to accommodate stitches. Do not join; work back and forth in rows.

Work decreases at armhole and neck edge 1 stitch in from the edge by slip, slip, knit (ssk) decrease at the beginning of the row and knit 2 together (k2tog) at the end of the row.

Back
With smaller needle and MC, cast on 107 (115, 119, 133, 139) sts.

Work 5 rows in Seed St pat.

Change to larger needle.

Row 1 (WS): Work 5 sts in pat, purl to last 5 sts, work 5 sts in pat.

Row 2 (RS): Work 5 sts in pat, knit to last 5 sts, work 5 sts in pat.

Rows 3–18 (20, 20, 22, 24): Rep [Rows 1 and 2] 8 (9, 9, 10, 11) more times.

Continue in St st only until back measures 11½ (12, 12, 12½, 12½) inches, ending with a WS row.

Armhole shaping
Bind off 6 (8, 9, 11, 7) sts at the beg of the next 2 rows—95 (99, 101, 111, 125) sts.

Dec 1 st at each side [every 4th row] 5 (7, 8, 10, 7) times—85 (85, 85, 91, 111) sts.

Work even until armhole measures 8¼ (8½, 8¾, 9½, 10) inches, ending with a WS row.

Mark center 37 (37, 39, 39, 53) sts.

Neck & shoulder shaping
Next row (RS): Bind off 8 (7, 6, 7, 9) sts, work to 3 sts before first marker, k2tog, k1, join 2nd skein of MC and bind off center 37 (37, 39, 39 53) sts; k1, ssk, work to the end of the row.

Next row: Working both sides at once with separate yarn, bind off 8 (7, 6, 7, 9) sts, work in pat across both sides.

Next row: Bind off 6 (7, 7, 8, 9) sts, work to last 3 sts, k2tog, k1; on next side, k1, ssk, work to end of row.

Next row: Bind off 6 (7, 7, 8, 9) sts, work in pat across both sides.

Next row: Bind off rem 8 (8, 8, 9, 9) sts, work in pat across both sides.

Next row: Bind off rem 8 (8, 8, 9, 9) sts.

Front
Work until front measures same as for back to armhole, ending with a WS row.

Armhole shaping
Bind off 6 (8, 9, 11, 7) sts at the beg of the next 2 rows—95 (99, 101, 111, 125) sts.

Dec 1 st at each side [every 4th row] 5 (7, 8, 10, 7) times—85 (85, 85, 91, 111) sts.

Work even until armhole measures 5¾ (6, 6¼, 7, 7½) inches.

Mark center 27, (27, 27, 27, 39) sts.

Shape neck
Work to marked sts, join 2nd skein of MC, bind off center 27 (27, 27, 27, 39) sts, work to the end of the row.

Working both sides at once with separate yarn, dec 1 st at neck edge [every other row] 7 (7, 8, 8, 9) times—22 (22, 21, 24, 27) sts.

Work even until armhole measures 8¼ (8½, 8¾, 9½, 10) inches.

Shape shoulders
Bind off at each shoulder [8 (7, 6, 7, 9) sts] once, [6 (7, 7, 8, 9) sts] once, and then, [8 (8, 8, 9, 9) sts] once.

House of White Birches, Berne, Indiana 46711   AnniesAttic.com

Finishing
Sew left shoulder seam.

Neck trim
With smaller needle, CC and RS facing, pick up and knit 3 sts for every 4 rows along right front neck shaping, in every st across front neck edge, 3 sts for every 4 rows along left front neck shaping, having same number of sts as along right neck edge, 3 sts for every 4 rows along back neck edge, in every st across back neck and 3 sts for every 4 rows across the right back neck shaping.

Knit 2 rows.

Change to MC and knit 2 rows.

Bind off loosely.

Sew right shoulder seam.

Armhole trim
With smaller needle, CC and RS facing, beg at underarm, pick up and knit in every bound-off st, 3 sts for every 4 rows around armhole and in each bound-off st at underarm.

Knit 2 rows.

Change to MC and knit 2 rows.

Bind off loosely.

Rep on other armhole.

Sew side seams, ending just above the Seed St border. ●

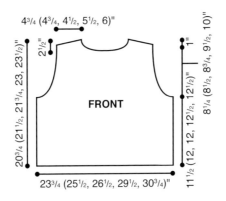

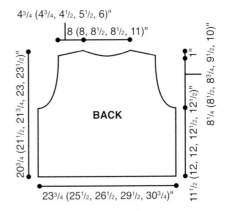

Swing Along

Expand your horizons with this jacket worked vertically. The slipped-stitch pattern creates a striking chain detail with contrasting yarn.

Design by Barb Kervin

. . . .

Skill Level
■■■■ EXPERIENCED

Sizes
Woman's 1X-large (2X-large, 3X-large, 4X-large, 5X-large) Instructions are given for smallest size, with larger sizes in parentheses. When only 1 number is given, it applies to all sizes.

Finished Measurement
Chest: 49 (51, 54, 57, 61) inches (after blocking)

Materials
- Conjoined Creations Lyrics Top Ten Collection (worsted weight; 100% silk; 105 yds/50g per skein): 7 (8, 9, 11, 12) skeins wild thing (MC)
- Conjoined Creations Surf's Up (DK weight; 59% soysilk/41% polyester; 200 yds/60g per skein): 3 (3, 3, 4, 4) skeins long board (CC)
- Size 9 (5.5mm) 24-inch circular needle or size needed to obtain gauge
- Stitch holders
- 5 (⅞-inch) buttons
- Stitch markers

Gauge
17 sts and 32 rows = 4 inches/10cm in Chained Striped pat, blocked.

To save time, take time to check gauge.

Pattern Stitch
Chained Striped (multiple of 8 sts + 6)
Row 1 (RS): With MC, knit across.
Row 2 (WS): Purl across.
Rows 3 and 4: With CC, knit across.
Row 5: With MC, k6, *sl 2 wyib, k6; rep from * across.
Row 6: P6, *sl 2 wyif, p6; rep from * across.

Row 7: With CC, rep Row 5.
Row 8: Knit across.
Rows 9 and 10: Rep Rows 1 and 2.
Rows 11 and 12: With CC, knit across.
Row 13: With MC, k2, *sl 2 wyib, k6; rep from * across.
Row 14: K2, *sl 2 wyib, k6; rep from * across.
Row 15: With CC, rep Row 13.
Row 16: Knit across.

Special Techniques
Short-row set: A set of short rows is worked in MC either before Row 1 and Row 9 at beg of RS row or after Row 1 and Row 9 at the beg of WS row as indicated in the instructions. On the following row, work the wrap tog with the wrapped st when knitting or purling across.

Provisional cast-on: With crochet hook and waste yarn, make a chain several sts longer than desired cast-on. With knitting needle and project yarn, pick up indicated number of sts in the "bumps" on back of chain. When indicated in pattern, "unzip" the crochet chain to free live sts.

3-needle bind-off: Hold sections of garment with RS tog, the tips of the 2 needles should be facing in the same direction. Using a 3rd needle, *insert needle into first st on front needle and then first st on back needle and knit these 2 sts tog; rep from * once more and pass first st on RH needle over 2nd st on RH needle. Continue in same manner until all sts are worked tog. Pull yarn through last st.

Pattern Notes
The back and fronts are worked from side to side. The provisional cast-on for the sleeve is in the sleeve-cap area of the sleeve; the pattern is then worked to 1 side of sleeve. The provisional cast-on is then removed and the pattern is worked to the other side of the sleeve. A circular needle is used to accommodate the stitches. Do not join; work back and forth in rows.

The set of short rows is worked throughout to create "swing" look at lower edge of sweater and sleeve. These rows are not included in row count.

Back
With MC and provisional cast-on method, cast on 62 (70, 70, 70, 78) sts.

Work 14 (14, 16, 18, 24) rows of Chained Striped pat, including short rows at beg of RS rows as follows: K24 sts, sl 1 wyif, bring yarn to back; turn, sl 1, purl back to beg of row.

Next row (RS): Work in pat to last 2 sts, inc, k1—63 (71, 71, 71, 79) sts.

Next row: Work in pat across.

Continuing in established pat [rep last 2 rows] 7 (7, 8, 9, 11) more times, working inc sts into pat—70 (78, 79, 80, 90) sts.

Work even in pat for 3 rows.

Next row (WS): Cast on 32 (32, 39, 38, 36) sts, work in pat across—102 (110, 118, 118, 126) sts.

Continue in established pat until back from armhole cast-on measures 18 (18, 18½, 19, 19) inches, ending with a RS row.

Next row (WS): Bind off 32 (32, 39, 38, 36) sts, work in pat across—70 (78, 79, 80, 90) sts.

Work 2 rows even.

Next row (RS): Work in pat to last 3 sts, k2tog, k1—69 (77, 78, 79, 89) sts.

Next row: Work in pat across.

Rep [last 2 rows] 7 (7, 8, 9, 11) more times—62 (70, 70, 70, 78) sts.

Work even for 14 (14, 16, 18, 24) rows, ending with a Row 2 or Row 10. Place sts on holder or waste yarn for finishing later.

Left Front
With MC and provisional cast-on method, cast on 62 (70, 70, 70, 78) sts.

Beg with Row 9 of Chained Striped pat, work even for a total of 14 (14, 16, 18, 24) rows, including short rows at beg of WS row as follows: P24, sl 1 wyib, bring yarn to front; turn, sl 1, knit back to beg of row.

Next row (RS): Inc st at beg [every RS row] 8 (8, 9, 10, 12) times—70 (78, 79, 80, 90) sts.

Work even in pat for 3 rows.

Next row (WS): At end of row, cast on 32 (32, 39, 38, 36) sts—102 (110, 118, 118, 126) sts.

Continue in established pat until shoulder measures 5½ (5½, 5½, 5¾, 5¾) inches from armhole cast-on, ending with WS row.

Neck shaping
Bind off at neck edge (beg of RS row) [8 (8, 11, 8, 11) sts] once, [4 (4, 5, 4, 5) sts] once, [3 (3, 4, 3, 4) sts] once, [2 (2, 3, 2, 3) sts] 3 (3, 0, 3, 1) time(s), [0 (0, 2, 0, 2) sts] 0 (0, 5, 0, 5) times.

Dec at neck edge every RS row [1 (1, 0, 1, 0) st(s)] 3 (3, 0, 3, 0) times—78 (86, 86, 94, 94) sts.

Work even until piece measures 12¼ (12¾, 13½, 14¼, 15¼) inches across front at underarm.

Change to CC and work 4 rows in garter st. Bind off loosely in garter st.

Right Front
With MC and provisional cast-on method, cast on 62 (70, 70, 70, 78) sts.

Beg with either Row 3 or Row 11 of Chained Striped pat, work even for a total of 14 (14, 16, 18, 24) rows, including short rows at beg of RS row as follows: K24, sl wyib, move yarn to front; turn, sl 1, purl back to beg of row.

Next row (RS): Inc 1 st at end [every RS row] 8 (8, 9, 10, 12) times—70 (78, 79, 80, 90) sts.

Work even in pat for 3 rows.

Next row (RS): At end of row, cast on 32 (32, 39, 38, 36) sts—102 (110, 118, 118, 126) sts.

Continue in established pat until shoulder measures 5½ (5½, 5½, 5¾, 5¾) inches from armhole cast-on, ending with RS row.

Neck shaping
Bind off at neck edge (beg of WS row) [8 (8, 11, 8, 11) sts] once, [4 (4, 5, 4, 5) sts] once, [3 (3, 4, 3, 4) sts] once, [2 (2, 3, 2, 3) sts] 3 (3, 0, 3, 1) time(s), [0 (0, 2, 0, 2) sts] 0 (0, 5, 0, 5) times.

Dec at neck edge every RS row [1 (1, 0, 1, 0) st(s)] 3 (3, 0, 3, 0) times—78 (86, 86, 94, 94) sts.

Work even until piece measures 12¼ (12¾, 13½, 14¼, 15¼) inches from armhole cast-on, ending with either a Row 4 or Row 12 of pat.

Mark placement of 5 buttonholes evenly spaced and centered in k6 portion of pat.

Next row (buttonhole): *Work in pat to marked k6 section, k2, k2tog, yo, k2 for buttonhole; rep from * across.

Next row: Work in pat across, purling yo's.

Change to CC and work 4 rows in garter st. Bind off loosely in garter st.

Sleeves
With MC and provisional cast-on method, cast on 94 (110, 110, 110, 110) sts.

Notes: Short rows are worked at beg of WS rows on 1 side and at beg of RS rows on other side for "swing" shape in cuff area.

Short rows worked across the length of the sleeve are used to shape the underarm area.

First side
Beg with Row 3 of Chained Striped pat work even in pat for 30 (32, 32, 32, 32) rows, including short rows at beg of WS row as follows: P12, sl 1 wyib, move yarn to front; turn, sl 1, knit back to beg of row.

Cap shaping
Bind off 2 sts at beg [every RS row] 12 (16, 16, 16, 16) times—70 (78, 78, 78, 78) sts.

Short-row set: With RS facing and MC, k10 (11, 11, 11, 11), wrap next st, turn, purl back.

Rep [short-row set] 6 (5, 5, 5, 5) more times, working over an additional 10 (11, 11, 11, 11) sts in each set and working wrap and wrapped st as you come to it on following row, then work short-row set over rem 0 (12, 12, 12, 12) sts.

Next row: Work across all sts.

Place all sts on extra needle or waste yarn for finishing later.

Second side
Removing provisional cast-on, place live sts on needle, working in pat including short rows at beg of RS row as follows: K12, sl 1 wyib, bring yarn to front; turn, sl 1, purl back to beg of row.

Cap shaping
Bind off 2 sts at beg [every WS row] 12 (16, 16, 16, 16) times—70 (78, 78, 78, 78) sts.

Short-row set: With WS facing and MC, p10 (11, 11, 11, 11), wrap next st, turn, knit back.

Rep [short-row set] 6 (5, 5, 5, 5) more times, working over an additional 10 (11, 11, 11, 11) sts in each set and working wrap and wrapped st as you come to it on following row, then work short row set over rem 0 (12, 12, 12, 12) sts.

Next row: Work across all sts.

Place all sts on extra needle or waste yarn for finishing later.

Assembly
Block to measurements. Sew shoulder seams.

Pick up live side seam sts, removing provisional cast-on. With WS tog, join seam using 3-needle bind-off.

Rep for other side seam and underarm sleeve seams. Sew in sleeves.

Finishing

Neck trim
With CC, pick up and knit 108 (114, 115, 127, 127) sts evenly around neckline.

Knit 3 rows. Bind off.

Sew buttons opposite buttonholes. ●

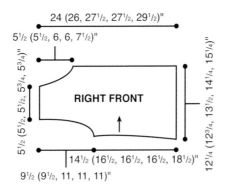

24 (26, 27½, 27½, 29½)"
5½ (5½, 6, 6, 7½)"
5½ (5½, 5½, 5¾, 5¾)"
RIGHT FRONT
12¼ (12¾, 13½, 14¼, 15¼)"
14½ (16½, 16½, 16½, 18½)"
9½ (9½, 11, 11, 11)"

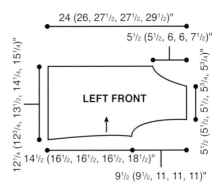

24 (26, 27½, 27½, 29½)"
5½ (5½, 6, 6, 7½)"
5½ (5½, 5½, 5¾, 5¾)"
LEFT FRONT
12¼ (12¾, 13½, 14¼, 15¼)"
14½ (16½, 16½, 16½, 18½)"
9½ (9½, 11, 11, 11)"

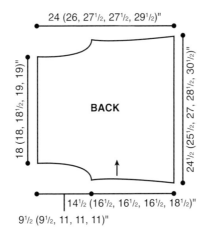

24 (26, 27½, 27½, 29½)"
18 (18, 18½, 19, 19)"
BACK
24½ (25½, 27, 28½, 30½)"
14½ (16½, 16½, 16½, 18½)"
9½ (9½, 11, 11, 11)"

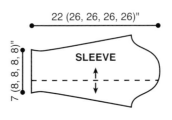

22 (26, 26, 26, 26)"
7 (8, 8, 8, 8)"
SLEEVE

Note: Arrow indicates direction of knitting.

Ipanema

Always a flattering garment, this wraparound cardigan will highlight the natural waistline of the wearer, as well as accentuate the bustline.

Design by Marlaina Bird

Skill Level

■■■□ INTERMEDIATE

Sizes

Woman's 1X-large (2X-large, 3X-large, 4X-large, 5X-large) Instructions are given for smallest size, with larger sizes in parentheses. When only 1 number is given, it applies to all sizes.

Finished Measurements

Chest: 45½ (50½, 55, 58½, 62½) inches, tied
Length: 26¾ (27¼, 27¾, 28¼, 28¾) inches

Materials

- Gedifra Samina (DK weight; 75% wool/25% nylon; 164 yds/50g per skein): 10 (10, 11, 12, 13) skeins charcoal #04393
- Size 8 (5mm) 24-inch circular and double-point needles (for I-cord) or size needed to obtain gauge

Gauge

21 sts and 29 rows = 4 inches/10cm in St st, blocked.

To save time, take time to check gauge.

Special Abbreviation

Make 1 (M1): Insert LH needle from front to back under horizontal thread between last st worked and next st on LH needle, k1-tbl (1 st increased).

Special Technique

I-Cord: With dpns, cast on 4 sts, do not turn; *slide stitches to other end of needle, pull yarn across back of work, k4; rep from * until cord is desired length. Sl 1, k3tog, psso, pull yarn through rem st.

Pattern Notes

Circular needle is used to accommodate stitches. Do not join; work back and forth in rows.

An applied I-Cord edging is worked along front and neck edges for stability and style. After the first few rows of the edging are worked, test the stretch and durability of the I-cord, which should be snug but should not cause edge to buckle. If edging is too tight, change to larger needle size.

Work all increases one stitch in from each edge by Make 1 (M1).

Work decreases 1 stitch in from edges. On right-side rows, work slip, slip, knit (ssk) at the beginning of the row and knit 2 together (k2tog) at the end of the row. On wrong-side rows, work slip, slip, purl (ssp) at the beginning of the row, and purl 2 together (p2tog) at the end of the row.

Back

With circular needle, cast on 126 (136, 148, 158, 170) sts.

Work in St st until back measures 2 inches, ending with a WS row.

Next row (RS): K1, ssk, knit to last 3 sts, k2tog, k1—124 (134, 146, 156, 168) sts.

Continue in St st and dec 1 st each side [every 4th row] 12 (12, 10, 10, 10) more times, then [every 6th row] 0 (0, 2, 2, 2) times—100 (110, 122, 132, 144) sts.

Continue even in St st for 15 rows.

Next row (RS): K1, M1, knit to last st, M1, k1—102 (112, 124, 134, 146) sts.

Continue in St st and inc 1 st each side [every RS row] 4 (6, 8, 8, 6) more times, then [every 4th row] 5 (4, 2, 2, 3) times—120 (132, 144, 154, 164) sts.

Continue even in St st until back measures 17½ inches from cast-on edge, ending with a WS row.

Armhole shaping
Bind off 8 (10, 10, 10, 11) sts at the beg of the next 2 rows, 5 sts at the beg of following 2 rows, then 3 (2, 2, 3, 3) sts at the beg of following 2 rows—88 (98, 110, 118, 126) sts.

Dec 1 st each side of [every RS row] 2 (4, 8, 9, 10) times, then [every 4th row] 5 (5, 7, 6, 6) times—76 (82, 86, 92, 98) sts.

Continue in St st until armhole measures 8¼ (8¾, 9¼, 9¾, 10¼) inches, ending with a WS row.

Mark center 14 sts.

Neck & shoulder shaping
Next row (RS): Bind off 5 (6, 7, 7, 8) sts, work to first marker, join 2nd skein of yarn and bind off center 14 sts, work to the end of the row.

Next row: Bind off 5 (6, 7, 7, 8) sts, work across to neck edge; on next side, bind off 4 sts, work to the end of the row.

Next row: Bind off 6 (6, 7, 8, 8) sts, work across to neck edge; on next side, bind off 4 sts, work to the end of the row.

Rep last row once more.

Next row: Bind off 6 (7, 7, 8, 9) sts, work across to neck edge; on next side, bind off 4 sts, work to the end of the row.

Bind off 6 (7, 7, 8, 9) sts at the beg of the next 3 rows.

Left Front
With circular needle, cast on 87 (92, 98, 103, 109) sts.

Work in St st until front measures 2 inches, ending with a WS row.

Waist, neck & armhole shaping
Next row (RS): Knit to last 3 sts, k2tog, k1—86 (91, 98, 102, 108) sts.

Continue in St st and dec 1 st at side edge [every 4th row] 12 (12, 10, 10, 10) more times, then [every 6th row] 0 (0, 2, 2, 2) times—74 (79, 85, 90, 96) sts.

Continue even in St st for 15 rows.

Next row (RS): K1, ssk, knit to last st, M1, k1.

Continue in St st and inc 1 st at side edge [every RS row] 4 (6, 8, 8, 6) more times, then [every 4th row] 5 (4, 2, 2, 3) times. *At the same time*, dec 1 st at front edge [every RS row] 18 (13, 11, 7, 7) times, then [every 3rd row] 25 (30, 30, 35, 35) times.

At the same time, when front measures 17½ inches from cast-on edge, on next RS row, bind off 8 (10, 10, 10, 11) sts once, 5 sts once, then 3 (2, 2, 3, 3) sts once. Dec 1 st at the beg [every RS row] 2 (4, 8, 9, 10) times, then [every 4th row] 5 (5, 7, 6, 6) times—23 (26, 28, 31, 34) sts rem after all shaping is completed.

Continue even in St st, if necessary, until armhole measures 8¼ (8¾, 9¼, 9¾, 10¼) inches, ending with a WS row.

Shape shoulder
Bind off at beg of next RS row [5 (6, 7, 7, 8) sts] once, [6 (6, 7, 8, 8) sts] once, then [6 (7, 7, 8, 9) sts] twice.

Right Front
With circular needle, cast on 87 (92, 98, 103, 109) sts.

Work in St st until front measures 2 inches, ending with a WS row.

Waist, neck & armhole shaping
Next row (RS): K1, ssk, knit to the end of the row—86 (91, 98, 102, 108) sts.

Continue in St st and dec 1 st at side edge [every 4th row] 12 (12, 10, 10, 10) more times, then [every 6th row] 0 (0, 2, 2, 2) times—74 (79, 85, 90, 96) sts.

Continue even in St st for 15 rows.

Next row (RS): K1, M1, knit to last 3 sts, k2tog, k1—74 (79, 85, 90, 96) sts.

Continue in St st and inc 1 st at side edge [every RS row] 4 (6, 8, 8, 6) more times, then [every 4th row] 5 (4, 2, 2, 3) times. *At the same time*, dec 1 st at front edge [every RS row] 18 (13, 11, 7, 7) times, then every 3rd row 25 (30, 30, 35, 35) times.

At the same time, when front measures 17½ inches from cast-on edge, on next WS row, bind off [8 (10, 10, 10, 11) sts] once, [5 sts] once, then [3 (2, 2, 3, 3) sts] once. Dec 1 st at the end [every RS row] 2 (4, 8, 9, 10) times, then [every other RS row] 5 (5, 7, 6, 6) times—23 (26, 28, 31, 34) sts rem after all shaping is completed.

Continue even in St st, if necessary, until armhole measures 8¼ (8¾, 9¼, 9¾, 10¼) inches, ending with a RS row.

Shape shoulder
Bind off at beg of next WS row [5 (6, 7, 7, 8) sts] once, [6 (6, 7, 8, 8) sts] once, then [6 (7, 7, 8, 9) sts] twice.

Sleeve

With circular needle, cast on 94 (102, 110, 116, 120) sts.

Work in St st until sleeve measures 3 inches, ending with a WS row.

Next row (RS): K1, ssk, knit to last 3 sts, k2tog, k1—92 (100, 108, 114, 118) sts.

Continue in St st and dec 1 st at side edges [every 8th row] twice, then [every 10th row] twice—84 (92, 100, 106, 110) sts.

Continue even in St st until sleeve measures 18 inches from cast-on edge, ending with a WS row.

Sleeve cap shaping

Bind off 8 (10, 10, 10, 11) sts at the beg of next 2 rows, 5 sts at the beg of following 2 rows, then 3 (2, 2, 3, 3) sts at the beg of following 2 rows—52 (58, 66, 70, 72) sts.

Dec 1 st each side on [every RS row] 2 (4, 8, 9, 10) times, [every 4th row] 6 (6, 4, 5, 5) times, then [every RS row] twice—32 (34, 38, 38, 38) sts.

Bind off 3 sts at the beg of the next 2 rows, then 2 sts at the beg of following 2 rows—22 (24, 28, 28, 28) sts.

Bind off all sts on next RS row.

Finishing

Block all pieces. Sew shoulder seams.

Front & neck I-cord edging

With dpns, cast on 4 sts. Beg at lower right front edge and work attached I-cord as follows: *K3, sl 1 to RH needle, insert tip of RH needle into edge st, and k2tog (slipped st and picked-up st), slip all 4 sts back to other end of needle, pull yarn across back of work; rep from * around neck edge and along left front to lower edge.

Bind off 4 sts.

Sew sleeves into armholes. Sew sleeve and side seams.

I-cord ties

Make 3 I-cords 15 inches long (see Special Technique). Make 1 more I-cord 44 (48, 52, 56, 60) inches long.

Referring to photo, sew one 15-inch I-cord at each front edge at beg of neck shaping and rem 15-inch I-cord to inside of left side seam (right front and inside left are tied together for closure). Sew longer I-cord to RS of right side seam. Tie short cord at inside of left side seam with cord at right front edge. Wrap long cord across front and around back of body, back to right side seam, and tie with short cord on right front edge. ●

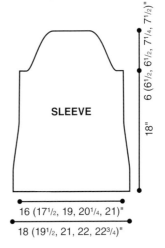

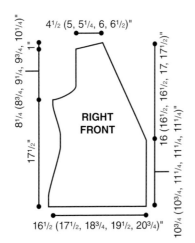

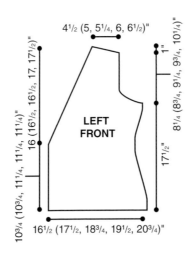

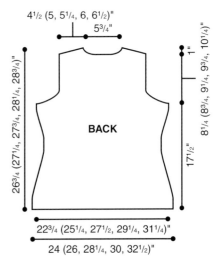

General Information

Abbreviations & Symbols

[ ] work instructions within brackets as many times as directed

( ) work instructions within parentheses in the place directed

** repeat instructions following the asterisks as directed

* repeat instructions following the single asterisk as directed

" inch(es)

approx approximately
beg begin/beginning
CC contrasting color
ch chain stitch
cm centimeter(s)
cn cable needle
dec decrease/decreases/decreasing
dpn(s) double-point needle(s)
g gram
inc increase/increases/increasing

k knit
k2tog knit 2 stitches together
LH left hand
lp(s) loop(s)
m meter(s)
M1 make one stitch
MC main color
mm millimeter(s)
oz ounce(s)
p purl
pat(s) pattern(s)
p2tog purl 2 stitches together
psso pass slipped stitch over
p2sso pass 2 slipped stitches over
rem remain/remaining
rep repeat(s)
rev St st reverse stockinette stitch
RH right hand
rnd(s) rounds
RS right side
skp slip, knit, pass stitch over—one stitch decreased

sk2p slip 1, knit 2 together, pass slip stitch over the knit 2 together—2 stitches have been decreased
sl slip
sl 1k slip 1 knitwise
sl 1p slip 1 purlwise
sl st slip stitch(es)
ssk slip, slip, knit these 2 stitches together—a decrease
st(s) stitch(es)
St st stockinette stitch/stocking stitch
tbl through back loop(s)
tog together
WS wrong side
wyib with yarn in back
wyif with yarn in front
yd(s) yard(s)
yfwd yarn forward
yo yarn over

Skill Levels

BEGINNER

Beginner projects for first-time knitters using basic stitches. Minimal shaping.

EASY

Easy projects using basic stitches, repetitive stitch patterns, simple color changes and simple shaping and finishing.

INTERMEDIATE

Intermediate projects with a variety of stitches, mid-level shaping and finishing.

EXPERIENCED

Experienced projects using advanced techniques and stitches, detailed shaping and refined finishing.

Standard Yarn Weight System
Categories of yarn, gauge ranges, and recommended needle sizes

Yarn Weight Symbol & Category Names	1 SUPER FINE	2 FINE	3 LIGHT	4 MEDIUM	5 BULKY	6 SUPER BULKY
Type of Yarns in Category	Sock, Fingering, Baby	Sport, Baby	DK, Light Worsted	Worsted, Afghan, Aran	Chunky, Craft, Rug	Bulky, Roving
Knit Gauge Range* in Stockinette Stitch to 4 inches	27–32 sts	23–26 sts	21–24 sts	16–20 sts	12–15 sts	6–11 sts
Recommended Needle in Metric Size Range	2.25–3.25mm	3.25–3.75mm	3.75–4.5mm	4.5–5.5mm	5.5–8mm	8mm and larger
Recommended Needle U.S. Size Range	1 to 3	3 to 5	5 to 7	7 to 9	9 to 11	11 and larger

* GUIDELINES ONLY: The above reflect the most commonly used gauges and needle sizes for specific yarn categories.

Inches Into Millimeters & Centimeters
All measurements are rounded off slightly.

inches	mm	cm	inches	cm	inches	cm	inches	cm
1/8	3	0.3	5	12.5	21	53.5	38	96.5
1/4	6	0.6	5½	14	22	56.0	39	99.0
3/8	10	1.0	6	15.0	23	58.5	40	101.5
1/2	13	1.3	7	18.0	24	61.0	41	104.0
5/8	15	1.5	8	20.5	25	63.5	42	106.5
3/4	20	2.0	9	23.0	26	66.0	43	109.0
7/8	22	2.2	10	25.5	27	68.5	44	112.0
1	25	2.5	11	28.0	28	71.0	45	114.5
1¼	32	3.2	12	30.5	29	73.5	46	117.0
1½	38	3.8	13	33.0	30	76.0	47	119.5
1¾	45	4.5	14	35.5	31	79.0	48	122.0
2	50	5.0	15	38.0	32	81.5	49	124.5
2½	65	6.5	16	40.5	33	84.0	50	127.0
3	75	7.5	17	43.0	34	86.5		
3½	90	9.0	18	46.0	35	89.0		
4	100	10.0	19	48.5	36	91.5		
4½	115	11.5	20	51.0	37	94.0		

Glossary

bind off—used to finish an edge

cast on—process of making foundation stitches used in knitting

decrease—means of reducing the number of stitches in a row

increase—means of adding to the number of stitches in a row

intarsia—method of knitting a multicolored pattern into the fabric

knitwise—insert needle into stitch as if to knit

long tail cast on—method of cast-on where length of yarn about an inch long for each stitch is left at end before making first cast-on stitch

make 1—method of increasing using the strand between the last stitch worked and the next stitch

place marker—placing a purchased marker or loop of contrasting yarn onto the needle for ease in working a pattern repeat

purlwise—insert needle into stitch as if to purl

right side—side of garment or piece that will be seen when worn

selvage stitch—edge stitch used to make seaming easier

slip, slip, knit—method of decreasing by moving stitches from left needle to right needle and working them together

slip stitch—an unworked stitch slipped from left needle to right needle, usually as if to purl

work even—continue to work in the pattern as established without working any increases or decreases

work in pattern as established—continue to work following the pattern stitch as it has been set up or established on the needle, working any increases or decreases in such a way that the established pattern remains the same

yarn over—method of increasing by wrapping the yarn over the right needle without working a stitch

Knitting Basics

Cast-On

Leaving an end about an inch long for each stitch to be cast on, make a slip knot on the right needle.

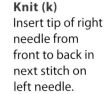

Place the thumb and index finger of your left hand between the yarn ends with the long yarn end over your thumb, and the strand from the skein over your index finger. Close your other fingers over the strands to hold them against your palm. Spread your thumb and index fingers apart and draw the yarn into a "V."

Place the needle in front of the strand around your thumb and bring it underneath this strand. Carry the needle over and under the strand on your index finger.

Draw through loop on thumb.

Drop the loop from your thumb and draw up the strand to form a stitch on the needle.

Repeat until you have cast on the number of stitches indicated in the pattern. Remember to count the beginning slip knot as a stitch.

Cable Cast-On

This type of cast-on is used when adding stitches in the middle or at the end of a row.

Make a slip knot on the left needle. Knit a stitch in this knot and place it on the left needle. Insert the right needle between the last two stitches on the left needle. Knit a stitch and place it on the left needle. Repeat for each stitch needed.

Knit (k)

Insert tip of right needle from front to back in next stitch on left needle.

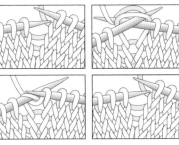

Bring yarn under and over the tip of the right needle.

Pull yarn loop through the stitch with right needle point.

Slide the stitch off the left needle. The new stitch is on the right needle.

Purl (p)

With yarn in front, insert tip of right needle from back to front through next stitch on the left needle.

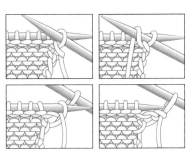

Bring yarn around the right needle counterclockwise. With right needle, draw yarn back through the stitch.

Slide the stitch off the left needle. The new stitch is on the right needle.

Bind-Off

Binding off (knit)

Knit first two stitches on left needle. Insert tip of left needle into first stitch worked on right needle and pull it over the second stitch and completely off the needle.

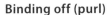

Knit the next stitch and repeat. When one stitch remains on right needle, cut yarn and draw tail through last stitch to fasten off.

Binding off (purl)

Purl first two stitches on left needle. Insert tip of left needle into first stitch worked on right needle and pull it over the second stitch and completely off the needle.

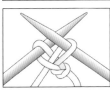

Purl the next stitch and repeat. When one stitch remains on right needle, cut yarn and draw tail through last stitch to fasten off.

Increase (inc)

Two stitches in one stitch

Increase (knit)
Knit the next stitch in the usual manner, but don't remove the stitch from the left needle. Place right needle behind left needle and knit again into the back of the same stitch. Slip original stitch off left needle.

Increase (purl)
Purl the next stitch in the usual manner, but don't remove the stitch from the left needle. Place right needle behind left needle and purl again into the back of the same stitch. Slip original stitch off left needle.

Invisible Increase (M1)
There are several ways to make or increase one stitch.

Make 1 with Left Twist (M1L)
Insert left needle from front to back under the horizontal loop between the last stitch worked and next stitch on left needle.

With right needle, knit into the back of this loop.

To make this increase on the purl side, insert left needle in same manner and purl into the back of the loop.

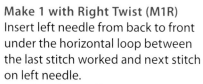

Make 1 with Right Twist (M1R)
Insert left needle from back to front under the horizontal loop between the last stitch worked and next stitch on left needle.

With right needle, knit into the front of this loop.

To make this increase on the purl side, insert left needle in same manner and purl into the front of the loop.

Make 1 with Backward Loop over the right needle
With your thumb, make a loop over the right needle.

Slip the loop from your thumb onto the needle and pull to tighten.

Make 1 in top of stitch below
Insert tip of right needle into the stitch on left needle one row below.

Knit this stitch, then knit the stitch on the left needle.

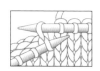

Decrease (dec)

Knit 2 together (k2tog)
Put tip of right needle through next two stitches on left needle as to knit. Knit these two stitches as one.

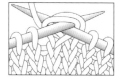

Purl 2 together (p2tog)
Put tip of right needle through next two stitches on left needle as to purl. Purl these two stitches as one.

Slip, Slip, Knit (ssk)
Slip next two stitches, one at a time, as to knit from left needle to right needle.

Insert left needle in front of both stitches and work off needle together.

Slip, Slip, Purl (ssp)
Slip next two stitches, one at a time, as to knit from left needle to right needle. Slip these stitches back onto left needle keeping them twisted. Purl these two stitches together through back loops.

Meet the Designers

. . . .

Mary Arnold

Mary comes from a varied background as a teacher, administrator and registered nurse. These careers contributed to her skills of creative problem solving, focus and discipline, organizational and process development, and creative presentations.

Color is her passion, fiber arts the medium. Learning to dye was the alternative when she could not find the "exact" expression in fabric for her quilting designs. She furthered her education in dyeing by following a course of study set out by the Handweaver's Guild of America.

Mary's husband and their 18 grandchildren keep her busy outside the workplace with designer pieces from Grandma Mary's inspiration. Mary resides in Cave Creek, Ariz.

Colleen East

Colleen comes from a career in the hospitality industry. She brings her analytical background and perfectionism to the fiber arts industry. There was once a time when Colleen sewed her complete wardrobe, and then she learned to weave, dye and spin. She now incorporates all these talents into her knitting, which she learned as a child, for hand-knit garment patterns and construction.

As a curvaceous woman, she learned to alter garments for plus sizes—a trick in itself—and shares some of her secrets and hints in this book. Colleen resides in Scottsdale, Ariz.

Barb Kervin

Barb Kervin has been designing for numerous indie dyers, along with designing extensively for Kollage Yarns. Her inspiration for designs are created with a better understanding of the needs of the knitters based on being a local yarn store owner for 19 years. Now retired on the central coast of California, she continues to expand her designs and knitting knowledge, focusing on the new fibers that are readily available to knitters.

Sharon Wittenberg

Sharon Wittenberg learned to knit when her next-door neighbor taught her in the attempt to stop Sharon from chewing her finger nails (yes, it worked!). She opened her own knitting store, Purls, in 1996 and expanded to two stores in 1999. Now retired, Sharon splits her time between Prescott and Tucson, Ariz.

Kate Lemmers

Kate Lemmers loves yarn. She loves to touch it, hold it, look at it, and of course, knit with it. Her designs are a blend of easy knitting mixed with beautiful accents to create garments that are classy, comfortable and timeless. Kate is currently living in the Poconos with her extremely understanding and supportive husband.

Amy Polcyn

Amy has been designing professionally since 2005. Her work appears regularly in major knitting magazines and in yarn company pattern collections. She loves designing projects that are simple to knit with an interesting twist. In addition to designing, Amy works as a technical editor for yarn companies, magazines and independent designers. Prior to casting off her day job for a full-time career in fiber, she worked for 10 years as an elementary school teacher. Amy lives in suburban Detroit with her husband of 15 years, 10-year-old daughter and 2 wool-loving cats. See what else Amy is up to at www.amypolcyn.com.

Marlaina "Marly" Bird

Marly is an avid crocheter and knitter who loves to share her passion with the students who attend her classes at local yarn shops. Balancing her day as wife, mom, podcaster, designer and teacher is a challenge, but Marly wouldn't change any of it! You can find more of her designs at www.thepurseworkshop.com and www.knitthing.blogspot.com.

Kristin Hansen

Although not an embryonic knitter, Kristin will admit to 40+ years of working with needle, thread and yarn. After a varied career, including obituary writer, software technical editor and visual effects producer, she and her husband "retired" to the mountains of Arizona. There, a life-long passion for fiber and crafts blossomed into a new career of Knitting Nanny patterns and classes.

Michael del Vecchio

Michael del Vecchio is creative director at Universal Yarn, and has been knitting and crocheting since 2001. In 2006, he released *Knitting With Balls: A Hands-On Guide to Knitting for the Modern Man*, and his designs and writing have appeared in knitting magazines and publications.

Resources

Many of the yarns presented in this book are available in your local yarn shop. If you should have any problems purchasing them in your area, the list below will serve as a helpful resource.

Berroco Inc.
14 Elmdale Road
P.O. Box 367
Uxbridge, MA 01569
(508) 278-2527
www.berroco.com

Conjoined Creations
P.O. Box 4110
Cave Creek, AZ 85327
(480) 488-0324
www.conjoinedcreations.com

Fibra Natura
Distributed by Universal Yarn
284 Ann St.
Concord, NC 28025
(877) UniYarn (864-9276)
www.universalyarn.com

Gedifra
Distributed by Westminster Fibers
165 Ledge St.
Nashua, NH 03060
(800) 445-9276
www.westminsterfibers.com

JHB International
1955 S. Quince St.
Denver, CO 80231
(800) 525-9007
www.buttons.com

Kraemer Yarns
P.O. Box 72
Nazareth, PA 18064
(800) 759-5601
www.kraemeryarns.com

Shawl pins available at
www.anniesattic.com.

HOUSE of
WHITE
BIRCHES
PUBLISHERS
SINCE 1947

Perfectly Plus is published by DRG, 306 East Parr Road, Berne, IN 46711. Printed in USA. Copyright © 2010 DRG. All rights reserved. This publication may not be reproduced in part or in whole without written permission from the publisher.

RETAIL STORES: If you would like to carry this pattern book or any other DRG publications, visit DRGwholesale.com.

Every effort has been made to ensure that the instructions in this pattern book are complete and accurate. We cannot, however, take responsibility for human error, typographical mistakes or variations in individual work. Please visit AnniesCustomerCare.com to check for pattern updates.

ISBN: 978-1-59217-317-4
1 2 3 4 5 6 7 8 9

Photo Index

21

24

36

28

32

40

44

48

53